first time
KNITTING

Creative Publishing
international

First published in the United States of America by
Creative Publishing international, a division of
Quarto Publishing Group USA Inc.
400 First Avenue North
Suite 400
Minneapolis, MN 55401
1-800-328-3895
www.creativepub.com
Visit www.Craftside.Typepad.com for a behind-the-scenes peek at our crafty world!

ISBN: 978-1-58923-805-3

10 9 8 7 6 5 4 3 2 1

Library of Congress Cataloging-in-Publication Data available

Technical Editor: Karen Weiberg
Copy Editor: India Tresselt
Cover Design, Book Design, and Page Layout: Megan Jones Design
Cover Photography: Lightstream

Printed in China

first time

KNITTING

THE ABSOLUTE BEGINNER'S GUIDE

by Carri Hammett

Creative Publishing
international

contents

introduction

WELCOME TO THE WORLD OF KNITTING! KNITTING IS SO MUCH MORE THAN JUST A WAY TO MAKE SOMETHING. YOU'LL SOON DISCOVER THAT THE PROCESS OF KNITTING IS RELAXING AND EVEN THERAPEUTIC. THE RHYTHMIC AND REPETITIVE MOTION IS VERY CALMING AND RESTFUL. MANY KNITTERS LOOK FORWARD TO THEIR QUIET TIME WITH NEEDLES AND YARN AS THE BEST PART OF THEIR DAY.

It doesn't require a big investment to learn how to knit. With this book, some yarn, and needles, you are ready to start learning. Your time investment isn't huge either. It only takes a few hours to learn the basic skills needed to make a simple scarf. Once you become hooked by knitting you'll find that you're eager to add new skills and make items with more complexity. The more you practice, the more confident you will become.

This book teaches you a range of knitting skills from the most simple, basic ones to more advanced techniques that will launch you confidently into the full spectrum of knitting options. Each chapter begins by teaching the skills needed to make the projects in that chapter. For each project you will find a list of the skills required and also the materials you will need.

You are always encouraged to make practice swatches so you can learn a skill before you use it on the yarn you choose for the finished project. Buy a skein of high-quality, worsted weight, wool yarn that knits at a gauge of 20 stitches = 4" (10 cm) (or 5 stitches to 1" [2.5 cm]). Choose a solid color that is a medium value (not too dark or too light to see details). You will also need a pair of single-point US size 8 (5 mm) knitting needles no longer than 9" (23 cm).

If you're an absolute beginner, then the best approach is to start with the first chapter and work your way through the book. Each chapter builds on the skills that were presented earlier. You don't have to make every project, but spend time learning the skills and in particular making the practice swatches. The first three chapters—Basic Knitting, Texture, and Shaping—will give you a solid skill set that will prepare you for the last two chapters—Knitting in the Round and Putting It Together—which offer new challenges and open new doors.

Let's get started!

BASIC KNITTING

Knitting is a versatile, easily transportable craft because the tools and materials are so simple; to get started you really only need yarn and knitting needles. The process of making a basic knit item is quite simple. In its most fundamental form, knitting requires only three steps: casting on, knitting, and binding off. You'll find that learning these three steps is easy. Then, by simply changing the needle size, yarn, or yarn combinations, you can achieve a variety of knitted fabrics suitable for different projects.

yarn

Yarn is simply a continuous strand of twisted fiber. The fiber can be anything from naturals like wool or cotton to luxury fibers such as cashmere and silk. You'll also find more unusual fibers such as bamboo, Tencel®, and linen and, of course, less expensive synthetic fibers such as nylon and acrylic. In addition, an abundance of yarns exist that are combinations of all the fibers available such as cotton/bamboo, wool/silk, or linen/acrylic. The selection can be mind boggling, so it may be helpful to find a good, independent yarn shop in your area. The local yarn shop (affectionately nicknamed LYS) is the perfect place to learn about yarn and find reinforcement for the skills that are taught in this book. Yarn shops are typically staffed by expert knitters who are eager to guide your success when you venture beyond what you've learned in this book. Good

craft or hobby stores and comprehensive online shops also carry a wide assortment of yarns, needles, and instructional materials.

TEXTURE

Yarn for handknitting comes in a variety of textures and different weights. In terms of texture, you'll find a wide range from smooth to wildly eclectic and bumpy. The photo below shows a range from left to right of smooth (merino wool), bumpy (cotton), boucle (alpaca/nylon), thick and thin (wool), fuzzy (mohair), chenille (rayon), eyelash (nylon), slub (nylon/metallic), and ribbon (nylon). The projects in this book use yarns that are primarily smooth or just a little bumpy because those are the ones that are most manageable for a new knitter.

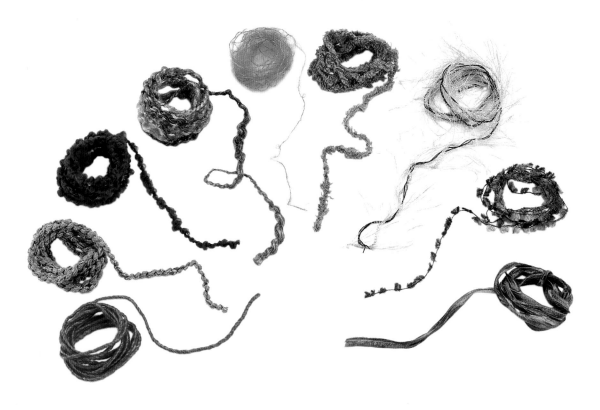

WEIGHT

Yarn is classified by the thickness or diameter of the strand and this classification is commonly referred to as weight. The thinner the yarn; the lighter its weight. The photo below shows a range of weights from super fine (fingering) to super bulky. On page 30 you will find an in-depth discussion of yarn weight and how to combine yarns for more variety in your knitting.

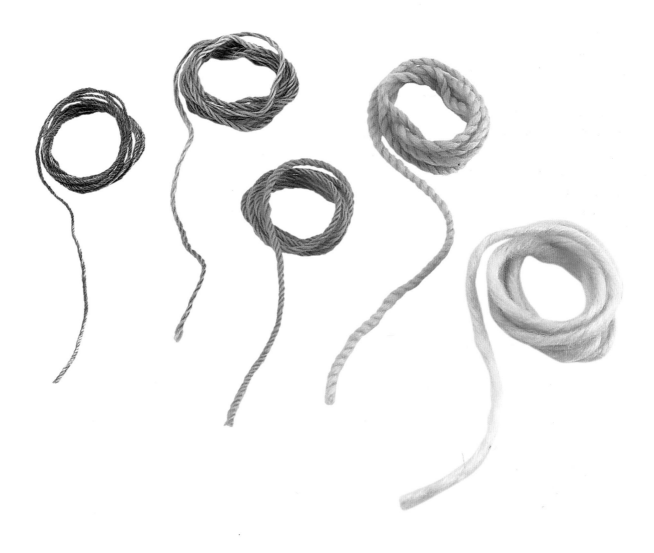

YARN PACKAGING

Yarn packaging (sometimes referred to as put-up) comes in a variety of forms. There are balls (they look like a doughnut) and skeins, which are densely wound and wrapped around the middle with a ball band (label). Both balls and skeins are ready to be used; simply pull the end out of the center.

Another common put-up is a hank which looks like a loosely twisted braid. It's very important to wind the yarn from the hank into a ball before you begin knitting, otherwise it will become tangled. Your LYS will often wind the yarn for you or let you use their equipment. If not, untwist or unfold the hank; you'll find it in a loose circle. Put both hands inside the circle and give a few good snaps outward, then drape it over the back of a chair or ask a friend to hold it. The yarn may be tied in two or three places to keep the hank from tangling. Find the ends and cut or untie the knots. Working with one end, wind the yarn into a ball.

YARN LABEL

Learn to read and interpret the information on a yarn label (also known as a ball band). You'll find some basic and predictable information such as the manufacturer, the country of origin, and fiber content. You'll also see the color number and/or name as well as the dye lot, which refers to the batch the yarn was dyed in. It's important to buy enough yarn to make your project, plus a margin for error, from the same dye lot. If you run out and have to purchase yarn from a different dye lot, then the color may not match, leaving a distinct line where the new dye lot starts.

Most yarn labels also include a distinctive square that gives information about the recommended gauge (number of stitches and rows per inch) and recommended needle size (page 15). Sometimes the square is omitted but you will always find needle and gauge information. The number of stitches per inch is an important number because it defines the weight of the yarn and lets you know whether the yarn is appropriate for the pattern you are using.

10 x 10 cm

4 x 4 inches

5 mm

8 US

28 R

20 S

Finally, you will see care information for the yarn expressed using a collection of symbols specifying how a garment made from the yarn can be washed and whether it can be ironed or dry cleaned.

TIP *Keep a journal of your knitting projects, and attach a yarn label and small yarn sample to each project page. You'll always have this vital information at your fingertips.*

CARE SYMBOLS

 Can be machine washed

 Hand wash in water temperature given

 Can be machine dried

 Do not machine dry

 Can be pressed

 Do not press

 Can be dry cleaned

 Do not dry clean

 Can be dry cleaned using "P" solvents

tools

KNITTING NEEDLES

Knitting needles come in three forms: single point (straight), circular, and double pointed. Needles are sized according to the diameter of the needle shaft, which is the same size regardless of the form (single point, circular, or double pointed). The patterns in the book will specify which type is required. The same advice that applied to purchasing high-quality yarn applies to needles. Don't buy the cheapest needles in the store, and don't use the long, heavy metal needles that were left to you by your great aunt. Follow these guidelines:

Single-point needles: As a new knitter you should use bamboo or wood needles no longer than 9" (23 cm) to 12" (30 cm). Old-fashioned metal needles can be very slippery and heavy and you might find your stitches slipping right off the end. Don't use long needles; they are unwieldy and can cause repetitive motion injuries. If your knitting won't fit on a shorter needle, then you should use a circular needle and knit back and forth (see page 48 or more information on this technique).

Circular needles: At first you may find bamboo circular needles easier to use because they aren't as slippery. You may find that the cable connecting bamboo needles is often in a stubborn, tight circle. Don't worry about this; the cable will loosen up as you knit. As soon as you feel confident and ready for the investment, switch to superior quality metal needles with supple cables.

Double-pointed needles: Look for bamboo or wood double-pointed needles that are 7" (18 cm) long because this is the easiest size for a new knitter to handle.

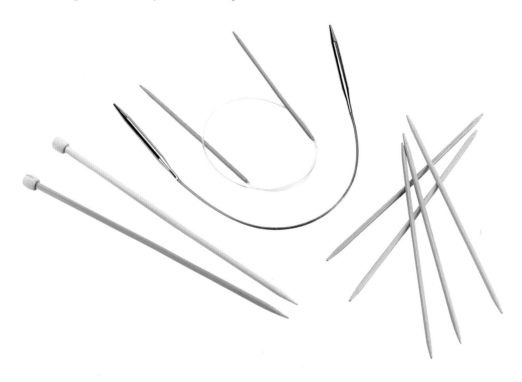

NEEDLE SIZING

As mentioned before, needles are sized according to the diameter of the shaft measured in millimeters (mm). Since needles are made and sold internationally, the markings can be confusing. Most commonly you will find the millimeter size and the equivalent US size. The most common US sizes range from 0 (2 mm) to 19 (16 mm). The other measurement is the length of the needle. The needle length is critical for circular needles and is measured from tip to tip (see page 86 for more information about common circular needle lengths).

KNITTING NEEDLE SIZES

US SIZE RANGE	MILLIMETER RANGE
1	2.25 mm
2	2.75 mm
3	3.25 mm
4	3.5 mm
5	3.75 mm
6	4 mm
7	4.5 mm
8	5 mm
9	5.5 mm
10	6 mm
10½	6.5 mm
11	8 mm
13	9 mm
15	10 mm
17	12.75 mm
19	15 mm

ESSENTIAL EXTRAS

There are a few other tools that every knitter should have: a tape measure, a yarn needle (distinguished by its curved point), stitch markers (both closed and locking), a needle/stitch gauge, and scissors.

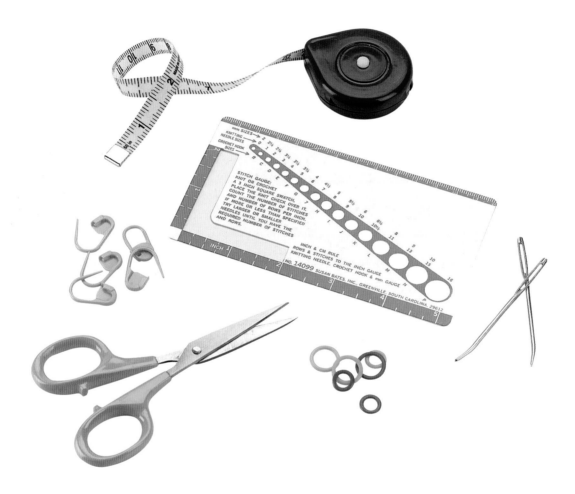

HANDY EXTRAS

As you progress with your knitting skill you'll find that you have more information to keep track of, which is where a row counter, calculator, and notebook come in handy. Stitch holders, cable needles, straight pins, and crochet hooks in multiple sizes are also useful tools.

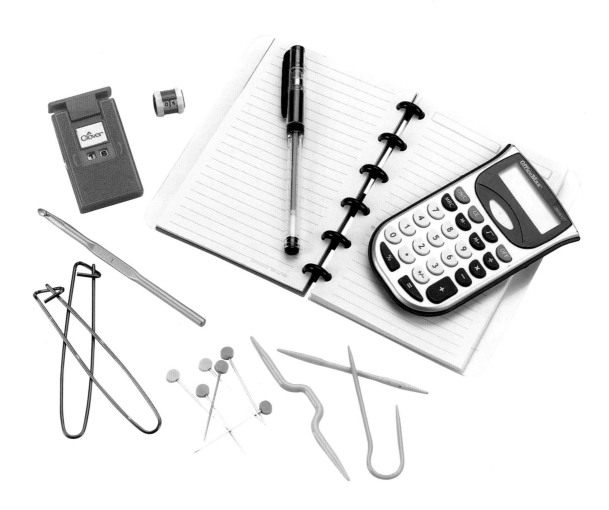

skills and useful information

TERMS

Take a moment to familiarize yourself with some common terms and definitions.

Casting on refers to the way stitches are first put on the needle. Think of this first row as the foundation for your knitting.

Long-tail cast-on is the technique used for most of the projects in this book. Its name refers to the long tail of yarn that is measured out before beginning and used to make the stitches.

Binding off (sometimes known as casting off) is how the final row of knitting is taken off the needles. Binding off creates a finished edge that will not unravel.

Knitting is what happens between casting on and binding off. It's the process of forming a continuous interlacement of loops that becomes knit fabric. There are two basic stitches that are used in the process of knitting, the knit stitch and the purl stitch. The first stitch any knitter learns is the knit stitch. It's a great stitch for making scarves, wash cloths, blankets, even garments. Later when you're ready to expand your skills, learn the purl stitch and techniques such as cabling and shaping.

Row is what is formed after knitting (or working) across all of the stitches on the needle. A row can be composed of all knit stitches, all purl stitches, or a combination of both.

Tail is the end of the yarn that is opposite the ball. It's also the residual length of yarn that is left behind after completing various knitting steps such as casting on, binding off, and adding a new ball of yarn or a different color.

Working yarn is the yarn that is coming out of the ball and what you are using to knit with.

SLIP KNOT

The first step to casting on is making a slip knot. Pull about 30" (76 cm) of yarn out of the ball. The slip knot will be made at a point that is about 24" (61 cm). The tail will be on the left and the working yarn will be on the right.

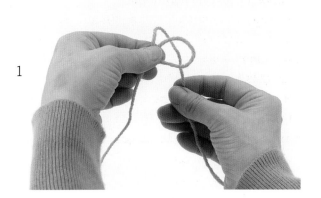

1. Make a clockwise loop with the working yarn on top and the tail on the bottom. Pinch the loop with the thumb and forefinger of your left hand and use your right hand to drape the working yarn behind the loop.

2. Holding the needle in your right hand, go under the strand of working yarn that is draped across the back of the loop.

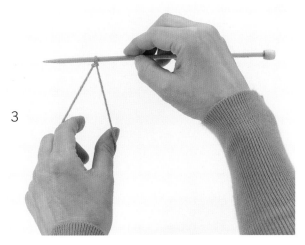

3. Drop the loop from your left hand. Pull the tail and the working yarn to adjust the tension and snug the loop on the needle The slip knot forms the first stitch on the needle when casting on.

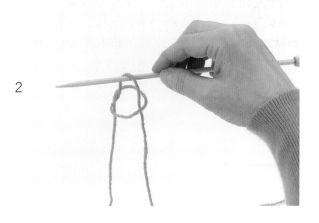

CAST ON (CO)

The most prevalent technique for casting on is known as the long-tail cast-on. It gets its name from the fact that half of the cast-on stitch is made using a tail of yarn, so before starting you must make sure your tail is long enough to cast on the desired number of stitches. A good rule of thumb is to allow about 1" (2.5 cm) for each stitch that is to be cast on. You can also wrap the yarn around the needle you'll be using once for each stitch and then add about 8" (20 cm) for good measure.

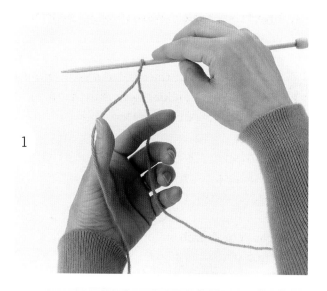

1   Start with the slip knot on the right needle. The tail should be about 24" (61 cm) long, which will allow for casting on about 20 stitches. The tail should be on the left and the working yarn on the right. Coming from behind, put the thumb and forefinger of your left hand between the tail and the working yarn. The tail should be draped over your thumb and the working yarn over your forefinger.

2   Use the other fingers of your left hand to hold both strands snugly against your palm. With the palm of your left hand facing you, spread your thumb and forefinger apart. The yarn will form a diamond.

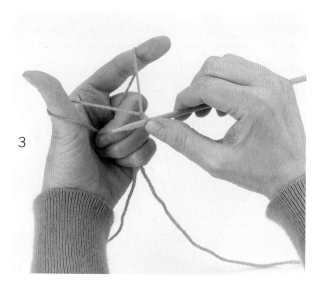

3   Pull the top of the diamond down with your right hand. Now it looks like a sling shot.

4 Insert the needle upward through the loop on the thumb.

5 Pivot the needle to the right and go over the top of and then under the working yarn on your forefinger, picking up a loop.

6 Pull the new loop down and through the thumb loop sending the needle back the same way it went in.

7 Drop your thumb out of its original tail loop, and then re-hook it on the tail to form the diamond again. A new stitch is now on the needle but it's too loose. Spread the thumb and forefinger of your left hand apart to gently pull the two strands at the base of the new stitch until it is snug (not tight!) on the needle. The second cast-on stitch is now complete. Reposition the yarn in the sling shot position and repeat steps 4 through 7 until you have memorized the motions.

5
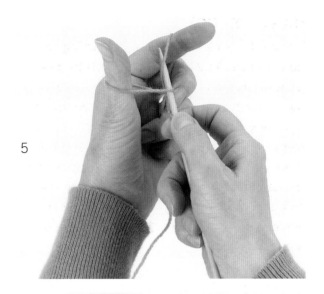

6
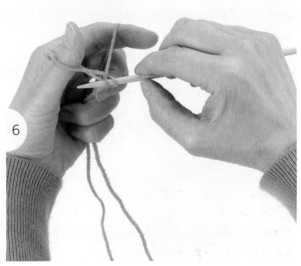

4
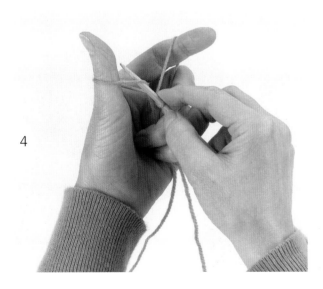

7

practice swatch

Knit (K, k)

Once you have mastered casting on, make a practice swatch using worsted weight yarn and US size 8 (5 mm) 9" (23 cm) single-pointed needles. Cast on 20 stitches and follow these steps to learn the knit stitch.

1 Hold the needle with the cast-on stitches in your left hand with the needle tip pointing to the right. As you work across the row the stitches will be transferred from the left needle to the right needle. The row is complete when all the stitches have been transferred off the left needle and onto the right needle.

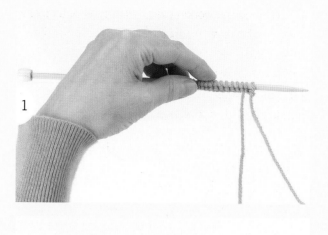

2 Hold the empty needle in your right hand with the tip pointing to the left. For both needles, your thumb and middle finger will be lightly grasping the needles. Working from the front to the back, insert the right needle into the first stitch on the left needle (the one closest to the tip) going through the loop just above the bump. The working yarn will be in back of both needles.

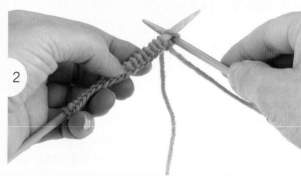

3 Use the fingers of your left hand to hold the needles so they form an X (the right needle will be in back).

4 Pick up the working yarn with your right hand and wrap it around the right-hand needle in a counterclockwise direction. The yarn will end up between the two needles. Later you will learn some special techniques for grasping the working yarn. For now, simply hold the working yarn between the thumb and forefinger of your right hand when called for.

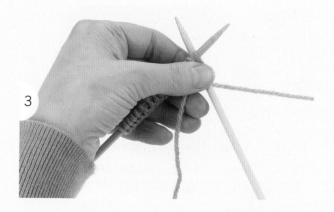

5 Holding the working yarn (with a bit of tension) and the right needle together, dip the needle down to the left and then toward you, drawing the working yarn through the first stitch on the left needle. The right needle will now be in front of the left needle with a new loop of yarn on it.

6 Slide the right needle to the right and off the end of the left needle, taking the newly formed stitch off the left needle. The original stitch will come with it. One knit stitch has been completed.

7 Repeat steps 2 through 6 across the remainder of the stitches on the left needle. One knit row has been completed. Notice that the right needle is now the "full" needle.

8 Transfer the right needle to your left hand with the tip pointing to the right to begin a new row. Before beginning the new row, gently tug at the bumps at the bottom of the new stitches and make sure the working yarn is coming out of the bottom of the bump on the stitch closest to the left needle tip. Repeat steps 2 through 6 across the row.

9 Continue working new rows on your practice swatch until you are comfortable with making knit stitches. The style of knitting you've just learned, with the right hand wrapping the yarn around the needle, is known as the English method. You will find information about the Continental method of knitting, which uses the left hand to wrap the yarn around the needle, on page 51.

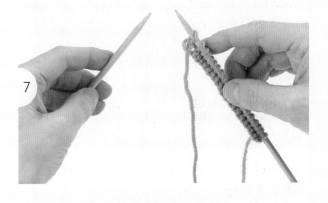

BIND OFF (BO)

If you were to remove your knitting from the needles before binding it off, the stitches would unravel. Binding off (also known as casting off) is how the final row of knitting is taken off the needle. Binding off creates a finished edge that is most often quite simple but can also be decorative. In this section you'll be learning the basic, simple version of binding off.

1. Knit two stitches onto the right needle in the usual way.

2. Use the left needle to lift up the stitch that is furthest away from the right needle tip (the first stitch that was knit).

3. Pass the lifted stitch over the stitch that is closest to the right needle tip (the second stitch that was knit) and off the tip of the needle. It's a lot like playing leapfrog with the stitches. When you are first learning to bind off you may find it easier to lift the stitch with the fingers of your left hand.

4. Knit another stitch onto the right needle and once again pass the second stitch on the right needle over the first stitch and off the end of the needle. Continue in this manner across the row until just 1 stitch is left on the right needle and the left needle is empty.

5. Cut the yarn leaving a tail at least 8" (20 cm) long. Remove the needle from the last stitch and pull on the loop to enlarge the stitch a bit. Reach through the loop with your thumb and forefinger, grab the tail, and pull it back through the loop. Continue pulling until the loop shrinks and is snug against the knitting.

JOINING NEW YARN

As you knit a longer scarf requiring more than one ball of yarn, you will need to join a new ball of yarn. The most important thing to remember is that you must leave a tail at least 8" (20 cm) long that can be woven in when you finish knitting. The best place to join yarn is on a selvedge (side edge), so plan ahead. Simply stop knitting with the old ball of yarn at the end of one row and start knitting with the new ball at the beginning of the next row.

If your yarn isn't too thick you can actually tie the new yarn to the tail of the old yarn at the beginning of a new row. Use the new yarn to tie an overhand knot around the tail and then slide the knot until it rests firmly against the edge of your knitting. Don't pull the bump through the stitch—leave it resting along the edge. You most certainly should use this technique with very slippery yarn.

When knitting with bulky yarn, simply stop knitting with the old ball of yarn at the end of one row and start the new ball on the next row. Some knitters worry about this method since it looks like it might unravel your knitting. You can tie half a square knot to hold the two tails in place until you finish, but untie the knot before weaving in the ends so you don't add a bump.

WEAVING IN ENDS

When your project is completed, the yarn tails must be secured. DON'T CUT THE TAILS BEFORE WEAVING THEM INTO YOUR KNITTING!

The tails can be woven into the cast-on edge, the bound-off edge, or the side (selvedge edge) of the knitting for items such as a scarf or blanket. If you're making a garment, weave the tails invisibly into the body of the knitting on the wrong side, either horizontally or diagonally.

To prepare the tail:

- Pull the tail to tighten up any loops or stitches that it's coming from.

- Thread the tail onto a blunt ended yarn

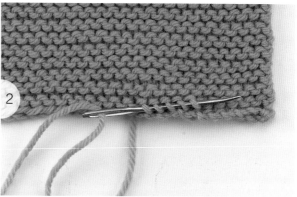

Weaving Tails along the Cast-On or Bound-Off Edge

1 Pass (or weave) the needle through the knit loops along the top or bottom edge for about 2" (5 cm).

2 Turn and weave the tail back in the opposite direction for about 1" (2.5 cm). Use different loops for the second, shorter section.

Weaving Tails along the Side (Selvedge Edge)

3 Pass (or weave) the needle through the loops along the side edge for about 2" (5 cm). Then turn and weave the tail back in the opposite direction for about 1" (2.5 cm). If possible, use different loops for the second, shorter section.

Weaving Ends Horizontally in the Body of the Knitting

4 On the wrong side of the knitting, weave the needle through the bumps or loops, working one loop at a time for about 2" (5 cm).

5 Then turn and weave the tail back in the opposite direction for about 1" (2.5 cm) through the loops on the opposite side of the row.

Weaving Ends Diagonally in the Body of the Knitting

6 On the wrong side of the knitting, weave the needle diagonally through the bumps or loops, working one loop at a time for about 2" (5 cm). Always weave through the bottom loop of the paired loops from each row.

7 Turn the knitting and weave in the opposite diagonal direction for about 1" (2.5 cm).

Finally, keep these guidelines in mind when you are weaving in ends:

- It's best to change yarn on the side edge. Avoid changing yarn in the middle of a row.

- Don't split the plies of the yarn when weaving the ends. Rather, go through the loops in the knitting.

- Whenever possible weave the ends into an area made from the same color.

- Frequently check the right side to make certain the weaving cannot be seen.

- When you have finished, gently pull the knitting in the direction of the woven-in tails to make sure the knit fabric isn't restricted. Trim the tails to ¼" (6 mm).

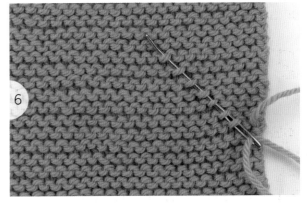

GARTER STITCH

Garter stitch is the simplest knitting stitch. It is created when all stitches and all rows are made using the knit stitch. Garter stitch looks the same on both sides and it is characterized by garter ridges, which can be seen clearly if the swatch is stretched a bit lengthwise (between the cast-on and bound off edges). The garter ridge is a bumpy, horizontal line extending between the two side edges of the knitting. The bumps are the interlacement of 2 rows of knitting. When counting knitting rows in garter stitch, each ridge represents 2 rows.

Garter stitch is an excellent stitch for a scarf. The fabric is dense, perfectly flat, and its edges don't curl. The simple structure of the stitch allows the yarn to be the focus. It stretches more in length than crosswise, and a scarf made using garter stitch should not be stored hanging but rather folded and left on a shelf.

HOW TO MAKE A GAUGE SWATCH

First of all, what is a gauge swatch? A gauge swatch is simply a small sample of knitting that is made to determine the width and height of your stitches, otherwise known as the gauge. You may wonder why it's important to make a gauge swatch. If you want the item you are making to turn out the way you expect and match the measurements specified in the pattern, then your stitches must be the same size as specified in the pattern. The pattern will tell you what gauge you need to achieve and it will be stated as the number of stitches (and sometimes rows) in an area of knitting that is 4" (10 cm) square. For instance, in the pattern for the Garter Stitch Scarf the gauge is 14 stitches = 4" (10 cm). Gauge can also be referred to as stitches to 1" (2.5 cm), which is simply 14 stitches divided by 4, or $3\frac{1}{2}$ stitches per 1" (2.5 cm).

To make a gauge swatch, use the needles recommended in the pattern and cast on the number of stitches in the gauge swatch plus two to four. Since the edge stitches are usually uneven, the gauge should be measured at least 1 or 2 stitches in from the edge. Knit at least 4" (10 cm) in the stitch pattern specified for the gauge in the project instructions. It's important that you make your swatch using the stitch specified. Don't be tempted to measure the swatch after just a few rows of knitting. It's important to "settle in" to your knitting with the new yarn and needles.

What if your swatch doesn't match the size specified in the knitting? If the swatch is wider than 4" (10 cm) then your stitches are too big. If the swatch is narrower than 4" (10 cm) then your stitches are too small. If your stitches are too big, then you need to use smaller needles; if your stitches are too small, then you need to use larger needles.

The most important thing to learn about gauge is that you don't have to use the needle that is called for in the pattern. Every knitter is different. Some are loose knitters, some knit perfectly to gauge, and some are tight knitters. Don't try to change your knitting style, which will only make you unhappy and hurt your hands. Change your needle size instead. Continue swatching with larger or smaller needles until your gauge matches that which is called for in the pattern.

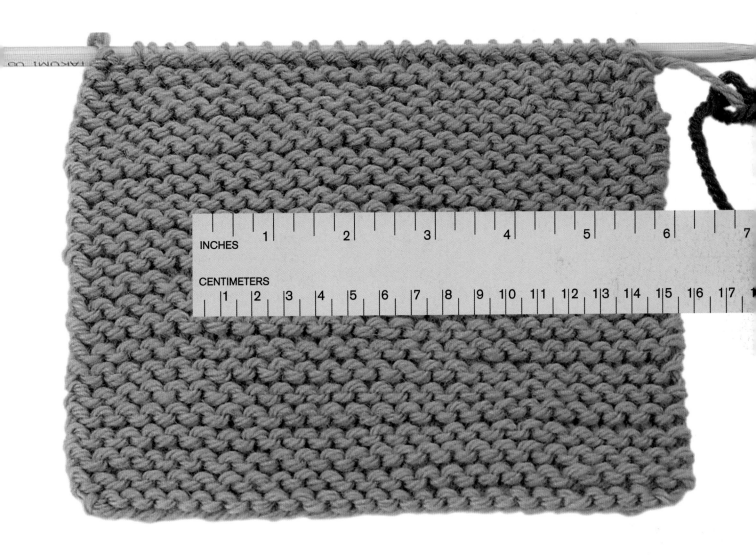

COMBINING YARN

You can change the look of a scarf by knitting with two or more yarns together at the same time. Yarn is typically classified by the thickness or diameter of the strand and this classification is commonly referred to as weight. Don't confuse the weight in terms of thickness compared to the total actual weight of the yarn ball or skein (usually 1.75 oz [50 g] or 3.5 oz [100 g]). The thickness, or weight, of yarn translates into how many stitches can be fit into an inch of knitting, and it also dictates how big the diameter of the needle shank should be.

You will often hear a yarn's weight referred to using traditional terminology such as fingering, sport, worsted, and so on. In the United States, the Craft Yarn Council has encouraged the use of a uniform standard of yarn measurement. Knitters have remained somewhat stubborn and often continue to use the traditional names. The most important information you need to know about a yarn's weight is stitches per inch.

As you gain experience as a knitter you will become familiar with the best use for a particular weight of yarn. The table at right gives information about current yarn classifications.

When two or more strands of yarn are combined the resulting yarn is, obviously, thicker. It helps to have an idea of the approximate weight of common combinations so you have a ballpark idea of what needle to use. Refer to the table at right for some common combinations.

The best combinations of yarn are those that highlight differences while still complementing one another. Two examples are shown opposite. Mohair is a great addition to smooth yarn, giving it some fuzz and softness, but it's most effectively used when the two colors are coordinated (**A**). On the other hand, when combining two yarns of similar texture, contrasting colors can work beautifully. Also, if you fall in love with a yarn that seems too fine for a scarf, then combine two strands to make a chunkier yarn (**B**).

Explore your creativity using the huge range of yarns available at your LYS or craft store. Be brave! Put some yarns together and make a swatch to explore what combinations of texture and color you like. If the result isn't what you expected, take joy in the learning process and try a different combination. But save the yarn that "didn't make the cut"; another yarn will make the perfect partner sometime in the future.

(A) Mohair and smooth yarn

(B) Contrasting colors

CRAFT YARN NEEDLE COUNCIL DESIGNATION	TRADITIONAL NAME	TRADITIONAL USES	STITCHES PER INCH	US COUNCIL SIZE
0 Lace 0	Lace	Lace	8 to 10	000 to 1
1 Super Fine	Fingering	Sock, baby	7 to 8	0 to 3
2 Fine 2	Sport	Baby, colorwork	6	3 to 5
3 Light 3	DK (Double Knitting)	Indoor garments, colorwork, children	5½	5 to 7
4 Medium 4	Worsted most common yarn weight	All types of garments;	5	7 to 9
	Aran	Fisherman cable sweaters	4 to 4½	8 to 10
5 Bulky 5	Chunky	Outdoor garments	3½	9 to 11
6 Super Bulky 6	Bulky	Coat sweaters, hats, mittens	2 to 2½	11 and larger

YARNS TO COMBINE	EQUIVALENT WEIGHT OF COMBINED YARN	SUGGESTED US NEEDLE SIZE FOR COMBINED YARN
2 strands of fingering (super fine)	1 strand of DK (light)	5 to 7
1 strand of fingering (super fine) and 1 strand of sport (fine)	1 strand of worsted (medium)	7 to 9
2 strands of worsted (medium)	1 strand of chunky (bulky)	9 to 11
1 strand of worsted (medium) and 1 strand of chunky (bulky)	1 strand of bulky (super bulky)	11 and larger

KNITTING WITH TWO YARNS HELD TOGETHER

Pull a length of yarn from each ball that is long enough to cast on the desired number of stitches. For a scarf, about 3 ft (0.92 m) is usually more than enough. Line up the ends and then draw the tails through your fingers a few times so the yarns cling to each other.

1 Pinch the two yarns together and form a slip knot with both yarns. Your "yarn" now consists of one strand each of two different yarns.

2 Cast on the desired number of stitches, always using both strands of yarn together and treating them as if they were one strand.

3 When the right needle enters the loop of the stitch on the left needle it needs to go through both strands. Likewise, when wrapping the yarn around the right needle to make a stitch both strands should be wrapped together.

4 You will most likely be combining yarns that are packaged in different lengths and will run out of one yarn before the other. Follow the directions on page 25 for joining new yarn.

1

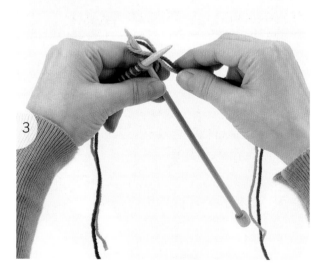

2

3

FRINGE

Fringe can be simple, made from the same yarn as the scarf, or it can be made using a completely different yarn in a contrasting color. The strands of yarn in the fringe can be consistent from one fringe section to the next, or you can mix up the strands. It's all up to you. If you plan to make the fringe using the same yarn as knit in the scarf, then plan ahead and set some yarn aside for the fringe before you start knitting.

Remember that the pieces will be folded in half after cutting. So, two cut pieces in a fringe section will actually make four ends.

1 Cut the fringe to twice the length desired plus 1" (2.5 cm). I often use a video dvd case: wrap the fringe around and around the desired number of times before cutting across the wraps on one end. Going around the long way makes a good fringe for a women's scarf and the short way is appropriate for children's and men's scarves.

2 Arrange the fringe pieces in bundles. The bundle will contain all the cut lengths for each fringe section. Fold the bundle in half.

3 Insert a crochet hook through the scarf on the edge where you want the fringe to be. Hook the fringe at the fold point and pull the fold through the scarf so that about half of the length is pulled through the scarf, forming a loop.

4 Reach through the loop with your fingers and pinch the cut ends, pulling them back through the loop (**A**). Gently pull the ends down until the loop tightens (**B**).

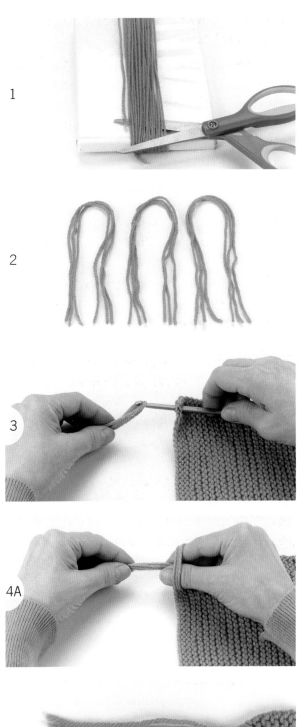

1

2

3

4A

4B

GARTER STITCH SCARF

The first project most knitters make is a simple garter stitch scarf. To make this scarf you'll be using a heavier weight yarn than what you use on the practice swatch. The heavier yarn will allow you to complete the scarf more quickly than if you were using worsted weight, and it's a good idea to start exploring different weights and types of yarn as soon as you feel comfortable with the basic knit stitch.

The yarn should be smooth in texture and a medium value solid color. Ideally, it should also be wool or a wool blend. Wool is far more forgiving for a beginning knitter because its natural elasticity makes it easier to maintain even tension.

The weight of the yarn for this project is known as bulky or chunky. This is a little bit on the thicker side but not so much that it's difficult to handle. When you shop for yarn, look for one that knits at 14 stitches = 4" (10 cm).

Choose a yarn you really like; don't try to save money by purchasing cheap yarn that doesn't excite you. If you don't like the yarn you probably won't finish the scarf, and for your first project success is really important! Also, keep it simple. Avoid yarn with bumps, loops, wild color variations, and fuzz.

MATERIALS

YARN
○ (5) bulky weight smooth yarn, approx. 230 yd (210 m)

NEEDLES AND NOTIONS
○ US size 10 (6 mm) 9" (23 cm) single-point needles or size needed to achieve gauge
○ yarn needle for weaving in ends

GAUGE
○ 14 sts = 4" (10 cm) in garter stitch

FINISHED DIMENSIONS
○ 68" x 5" (173 x 13 cm)

SKILLS

○ cast on
○ knit
○ bind off
○ weave in yarn ends

HOW TO KNIT A GARTER STITCH SCARF

1. Make a gauge swatch using the bulky weight yarn and US size 10 (6 mm) 9" (23 cm) single-pointed needles. Cast on 16 stitches and work every row in knit stitch (garter stitch) until the length from the cast-on row is at least 4" (10 cm). Measure your swatch from side to side, or parallel to the needles, and do not measure the edge stitches. If necessary, switch to different size needles and knit a new swatch until you achieve the correct gauge.

2. Cast on 18 stitches.

3. **Row 1:** Knit.

4. Repeat row 1 over and over until the length from the cast-on row is approximately 68" (173 cm) or desired length.

5. Bind off loosely and evenly.

6. Weave in loose ends to finish.

4

5

6

SCARF KNIT WITH TWO YARNS

This scarf is made by combining a bumpy bouclé yarn with a short eyelash/novelty yarn. The novelty yarn has a hint of metallic, which adds some intriguing sparkle to the bouclé yarn.

MATERIALS

YARN

○ yarn A: **(5)** bulky weight bouclé yarn, approx. 130 yd (119 m)

○ yarn B: **(3)** light weight novelty yarn, approx. 130 yd (119 m)

NEEDLES AND NOTIONS

○ US size 11 (8 mm) 9" (23 cm) single-pointed needles or size needed to achieve gauge

○ yarn needle for weaving in ends

○ crochet hook, US size K-10½ (6. 5mm)

○ pins for marking placement of fringe

GAUGE

○ 9 sts = 4" (10 cm) in stockinette stitch

FINISHED DIMENSIONS

○ 50" x 5¼" (127 x 13 cm) without fringe

○ 64" x 5¼" (163 x 13 cm) with fringe

SKILLS

○ cast on

○ knit

○ bind off

○ weave in yarn ends

○ knitting with two yarns at the same time

○ adding fringe

HOW TO KNIT A SCARF
MADE WITH TWO YARNS

1 Before you begin knitting, cut and set aside approximately 10 yards (9 m) each of yarn A and yarn B for the fringe. With yarn A and yarn B held together, cast on 12 stitches.

2 **Row 1:** With yarn A and yarn B held together, knit every stitch to the end of the row.

3 Repeat row 1 until the scarf is 50" (127 cm) or the desired length. Bind off all stitches loosely and evenly. Weave in loose ends to finish.

MAKE THE FRINGE

4 Cut 24 pieces of yarn A and 24 pieces of yarn B to a length of 14" (36 cm). Arrange 12 fringe bundles, each with two pieces of yarn A and two pieces of yarn B. Confirm fringe length.

5 Measure the end of the scarf and mark the fringe locations approximately 1" (2.5 cm) apart starting and ending at each corner. There will be a total of six fringe sections.

6 Using the crochet hook and following the general directions on page 33, attach one fringe section to each point marked by the pin.

7 If desired, trim the fringe to an even length using scissors or a rotary cutter.

4

5

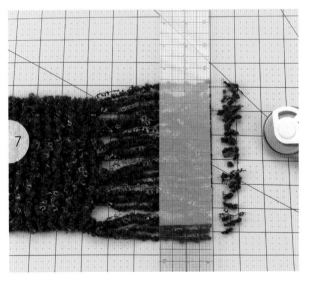

7

TEXTURE

The primary means of creating texture in knitting is combining knit stitches with purl stitches. Once you've mastered purling, a huge variety of stitches will open up for you. In this chapter you'll learn just a few: stockinette stitch, reverse stockinette stitch, seed stitch, and rib.

skills and useful information

So far you've learned how to cast-on, knit, and bind-off. There's one more essential skill to add—the purl stitch.

practice swatch

Purl (P, p)

Make a practice swatch using worsted weight yarn and US size 8 (5 mm) single-pointed needles.

1 Begin the practice swatch by casting on 25 stitches and knitting 1 row.

2 Hold the needles as you would for knitting but with the working yarn in front. The needle with the stitches on it will be in your left hand and the empty needle in your right hand. Working from the back to the front, insert the right needle into the first stitch on the left needle (the one closest to the tip), going through the loop just above the bump. (Some knitters find it easier to envision this step as inserting the needle from the right to the left.)

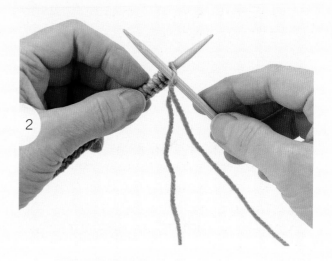

3 Use the fingers of your left hand to hold the needles so they form an X (the right needle will be in front).

4 Pick up the working yarn with your right hand and wrap it around the right-hand needle in a counterclockwise direction. Later you will learn some special techniques for grasping the working yarn. For now, simply hold the working yarn between the thumb and forefinger of your right hand when called for.

5 Holding the working yarn (with a bit of tension) and the right needle together, dip the needle down to the left and then away from you, drawing the working yarn through the first stitch on the left needle. The right needle will now be to back of the left needle with a new loop of yarn on it.

6 Slide the right needle to the right and off the end of the left needle, taking the newly formed stitch off the left needle. The original stitch will come with it. One purl stitch has been completed. Work several more rows of purl stitch until you feel comfortable with the movements.

practice swatch

Alternating Knit Rows and Purl Rows to Make Stockinette Stitch (St st)

Stockinette stitch is created when knit rows are alternated with purl rows. Continue on the purl practice swatch, but first mark one side with a safety pin or locking stitch marker. This will be the side on which knit rows are made; the side without the marker will be for purl rows. Work two rows as follows:

Row 1 (with marker): Knit all stitches.

Row 2: Purl all stitches.

Continue, repeating rows 1 and 2 over and over. Practice until you feel completely comfortable with stockinette stitch. Bind off.

THE DIFFERENCE BETWEEN A KNIT STITCH AND A PURL STITCH

Take a look at the swatch you just made and observe how the knit stitches and purl stitches have unique characteristics. The knit stitches (on the side of the swatch with the marker) form flat, vertical "V"s on the side facing you **(A)**. Purl stitches form horizontal bars or bumps on the side facing you **(B)**. The wrong side of the knit stitch looks like purl and the wrong side of purl looks like knit. The bumpy, purl side of stockinette stitch is called reverse stockinette stitch (rev St st).

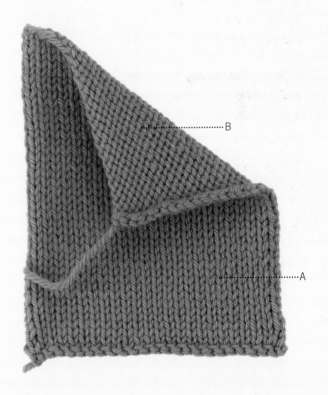

SWITCHING BETWEEN KNIT STITCH AND PURL STITCH IN THE SAME ROW

Texture stitches often require you to switch between a knit stitch and a purl stitch or a combination of stitches in the same row. When you are making a knit stitch, the yarn is in back of the needle; for a purl stitch the yarn is in front of the needle. When switching between a knit stitch and a purl stitch it is necessary to move the yarn back and forth **between** the needles, not over or around them.

Stockinette Stitch Needs a Partner

You will rarely see stockinette stitch used as the only stitch in a scarf. The edges of stockinette stitch curl, and a scarf made only from this stitch will turn in upon itself to form a long tube. To avoid this, you must use some other stitch to make the top, bottom, and sides of the knitting. Take the time now to make a practice swatch that will demonstrate how to control the edge curl of stockinette stitch.

practice swatch

Switching Between Knit and Purl in the Same Row

Practice switching between knit and purl on the same row by making a practice swatch using worsted weight yarn and US size 8 (5 mm) 9" (23 cm) single-pointed needles.

1 Begin the practice swatch by casting on 24 stitches.

Rows 1 to 6: Knit.

2 Now you will make the main area of the swatch by repeating two rows over and over. The swatch will have a border of garter stitch (knit on both sides) with a middle section of stockinette stitch (knit 1 row, purl 1 row). Before beginning these rows, read the section above about switching between knit stitch and purl stitch.

Row 7: Knit 4, move yarn between the needles to the front, purl 16, move yarn between the needles to the back, knit 4.

Row 8: Knit.

Repeat rows 7 and 8 until the swatch is almost square or until you've reached the desired length.

To finish, work six additional rows in garter stitch:

3 **Rows 9 to 14:** Knit.

Bind off.

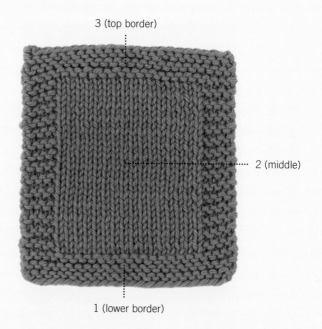

3 (top border)

2 (middle)

1 (lower border)

CABLE CAST-ON

The baby blanket pattern (page 57) requires that you cast on 144 stitches. It's frustrating to get almost finished with casting on using the long-tail method, only to discover that your tail is too short to complete all the required stitches and you need to start over. The cable cast-on can be used in place of a standard long-tail cast-on. It's also very useful for adding stitches at the beginning of an existing row. When used for the original cast-on it requires only a short tail, so you don't need to worry about estimating the length of the tail.

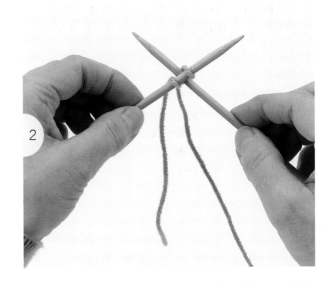

1 Begin by making a slip knot (page 19), leaving a tail about 8" (20 cm) long. Place the right needle into the loop made by the slip knot and wrap the yarn around as if you were making a knit stitch. Instead of leaving this stitch on the right needle, place it on the left needle.

2 Insert the right needle into space between the first and second stitch on the left needle.

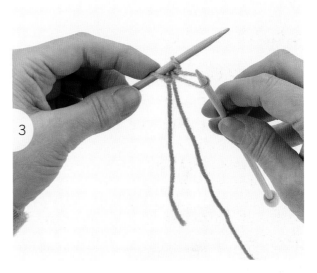

3 Wrap the yarn around the right needle and pull a loop through to the front as if you were knitting a stitch.

4 Place this new loop back onto the left needle.

5 Repeat steps 2, 3, and 4 until the desired number of stitches has been added. It is not necessary to switch the needle to the left hand after the cast-on row. It is already oriented to begin the first row of knitting.

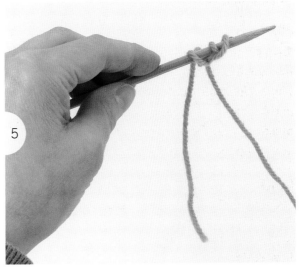

KNITTING FLAT ITEMS USING A CIRCULAR NEEDLE

Circular needles are most often used for knitting a cylinder, such as a sweater body or a hat, but they are also quite useful when the width of an item is much too large to fit on a straight needle. The solution is to knit back and forth on a circular needle. Think of the circular needle as two single-pointed needles that are joined together with a cable.

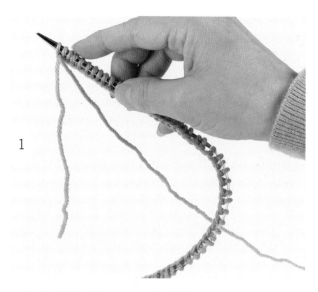

1 To cast on using the long-tail method, hold the needle in your right hand as usual. As you cast on more and more stitches, they will slide off the needle and onto the cable.

2 When you finish casting on, transfer the needle to your left hand with the needle tip pointing to the right. With your right hand, pick up the other end of the needle. Just ignore the cable and start knitting as always.

3 As with the cast-on row, the stitches will move off the right needle and onto the cable as you knit across the row.

4 When you finish the row, all of the stitches will have been transferred to the right needle. Switch again, putting the needle that's in your right hand into your left hand with the needle tip pointing to the right. Pick up the empty side of the needle and start the next row.

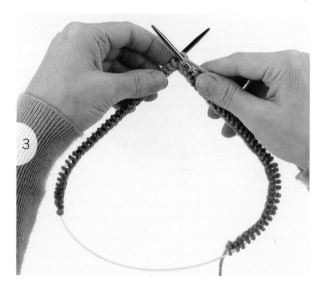

Casting on to a circular needle using the cable cast-on method is very similar except all the stitches will be cast on to the left needle and you will be using the right needle to make the cast-on loops. It is not necessary to switch the needle to the left hand after the cast-on row. It is already oriented to begin the first row of knitting.

STITCH MARKERS
Place Marker (pm)
Slip Marker (sm)
Remove Marker (rm)

Stitch markers can be very helpful in a pattern to mark the beginning and end of a set of stitches.

1 To place a marker (pm) simply slip it onto the right needle at the point indicated in the pattern.

2 When you reach a marker while knitting a row, slip it from the left needle to the right needle (sm) and continue with the next repeat.

3 When it's time to remove the marker (rm), simply take the marker off the left needle and set aside, then continue knitting without the marker.

READING PATTERNS

Brackets [ ] are often used in patterns as a short-hand way of expressing a repeated instruction. The brackets enclose a set of instructions such as [k12, p12] followed by the number of repeats required, such as 3 times. So, if you see the direction [k12, p12] 3 times, then you would k12, p12, k12, p12, k12, p12.

You will find a paired asterisk symbol (*) used in the patterns which indicates a repeat of the directions found between the asterisks (* *). Generally, directions between asterisks such as *K2, p2* are repeated over and over to the end of the row or until a specified number of stitches remain.

DAMP BLOCKING

Most knit items you make will need to be blocked. The process of blocking uses steam or moisture to even out and relax the stitches, smooth out the knit fabric, and straighten the edges. To a certain degree blocking can be used to make a piece of knitting conform to the intended shape, such as square or an angle in a garment piece such as a sleeve. Blocking can make an item somewhat bigger if desired but is not effective in making an item smaller. Certain types of knitting such as lace require blocking in order to make the stitches lie flat.

If the item you've made is delicate or the yarn contains nylon, then it's a good candidate for damp blocking. This method is also effective for an item that is too big for steaming on your ironing board.

Block the item in a sandwich of damp towels that have been immersed in water in your washer and then spun dry. Start by placing a damp towel on a blocking board, carpeted floor, or bed mattress. The towel should be wider and longer than the item you will be blocking; if necessary use more than one towel. Lay the item to be blocked on top of the wet towel and smooth it into shape. Use rustproof T-pins to pin the item to the blocking surface beginning with the corners. Use a tape measure to make sure the width and length are consistent or the item matches the dimensions and shape specified in the pattern. Continue by pinning all the edges at frequent intervals. Cover the entire item with a second damp towel. Leave the towels in place until the item is completely dry.

STEAM BLOCKING

If you don't have the time for damp blocking or if you are working on a smaller item, then steam blocking can be very effective. Keep in mind that this method uses hot steam and is not appropriate for any yarns that contain acrylic or nylon.

To steam block, hold the steam iron about 1" (2.5 cm) above the item and allow the steam to penetrate the fabric. In stages, set the iron aside and use your hand to smooth out the fabric and make sure the width is consistent. Also, pay careful attention to the edges, making sure they are straight and even. If the item you're blocking needs to be stretched or needs to conform to a particular shape, then use rustproof T-pins to pin into place on the ironing board. Leave the item on the board until it is completely dry.

HEIGHT AND WIDTH DIFFERENCES OF KNIT STITCHES

A knit stitch is wider than it is tall. This presents some challenges when attempting to knit blocks. In order to achieve a square shape there must be more rows (vertically) than stitches (horizontally) in a block. You'll see this in the baby blanket pattern on page 57. Each block is 12 stitches wide, but 18 rows are worked in order to achieve a square shape for each of the blocks. Keep this in mind when you start creating designs of your own.

HOW TO HOLD THE YARN AND NEEDLES—ENGLISH OR CONTINENTAL METHOD

There are as many ways to hold knitting needles and tension the yarn as there are cultures. However, there are two predominant methods, and they depend on which hand holds the working yarn; right hand for the English method and left hand for the Continental method. The English method is sometimes referred to as "throwing" and the Continental method is sometimes referred to as "picking." The hand you use to hold the yarn is not determined by which is your dominant hand. It's a matter of what makes you feel more comfortable, what you've been exposed to (how did your mom or aunt knit) and the specific task you are undertaking.

Generally speaking, the yarn is intertwined through the fingers and often wrapped around the little finger. You can see the English method below and the Continental method above on the left. The act of twining the yarn through the fingers keeps it organized, ready at hand, and gives it a bit of tension. If you learn to do this you will be able to knit much faster than when you pick up the yarn to wrap it for each individual stitch. You don't have to twine the yarn the same way as shown; if a different method works better for you then use it.

Continental method

English method

practice swatch

English and Continental Methods

Familiarize yourself with the two methods of knitting by making a practice swatch using worsted weight yarn and US size 8 (5 mm) 9" (23 cm) single-pointed needles.

KNITTING USING THE ENGLISH METHOD

All of the instruction to this point has been taught using the English method except that the yarn wasn't twined in the fingers; it was pinched between the thumb and forefinger.

With the English method it helps to insert the needle into the right stitch first and hold both needles with your left hand as you twine the yarn around your right fingers and prepare to knit or purl.

1 Cast on 25 stitches. With the yarn at the back of the needle, twine the yarn as shown (opposite, bottom), and move your whole hand to wrap or "throw" the yarn around the needle to make the loop for the stitch.

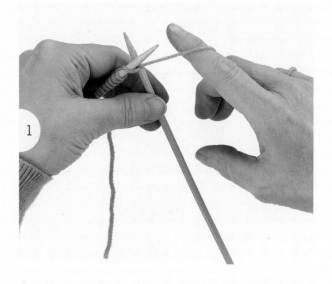

2 Instead of holding the yarn along with the needle to provide tension, allow the yarn to rest over the forefinger when pulling the new loop through the old stitch. Work a few rows on your swatch in knit stitch using the English method.

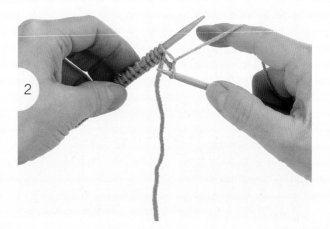

PURLING USING THE ENGLISH METHOD

3 Purling using the English method is very similar to knitting. Wrap the yarn through your fingers in the same manner but keep the yarn in front of the needles. Work a few rows on your swatch in purl stitch using the English method.

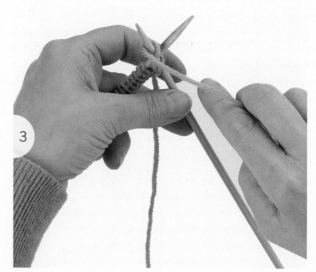

KNITTING USING THE CONTINENTAL METHOD

The Continental method will feel quite different to you at first if you've only used the English method. Many knitters find this method to be much faster but only after some practice.

1 To start, twine the yarn through the fingers of your left hand as shown on page 51, top. The working yarn should drape over the left forefinger with some tension. The yarn is held behind and no more than 1" (2.5 cm) above the left needle.

2 Insert the right needle into the first stitch on the left needle from front to back. Catch or "pick" a loop for the new stitch by moving the right needle over and then under the working yarn.

3 Pull this new loop through the stitch on the left needle and onto the right needle just like the English method. Work a few rows on your swatch in knit stitch using the Continental method.

PURLING USING THE CONTINENTAL METHOD

1 Twine the yarn around the fingers of the left hand as with knitting and hold the working yarn to the front of the needles.

2 Insert the right needle into the first stitch on the left needle from back to front. Cock your right forefinger down behind the right needle in order to lay the working yarn over and then behind the right needle.

3 Keeping tension on the loop, move the right needle to the back, and pull the new loop through the old stitch onto the right needle just like the English method. Work a few rows on your swatch in purl stitch using the Continental method.

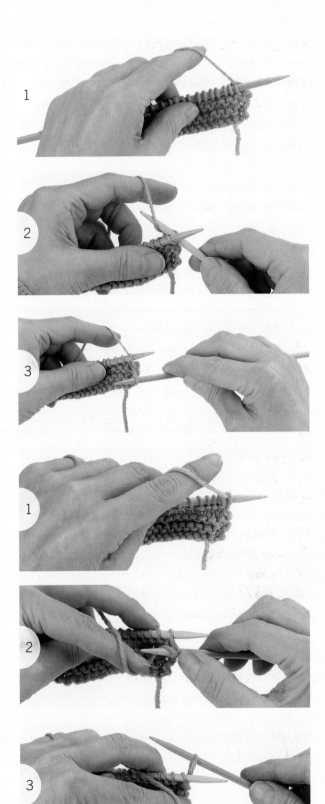

SEED STITCH

Many texture stitches will require you to switch between knit and purl every 1 or 2 stitches. One of those stitches is seed stitch, which is knit 1 stitch, purl 1 stitch alternating across the row. The important thing to remember about switching between knits and purls on the same row is to move the yarn between the needles to the front for a purl stitch and between the needles to the back for a knit stitch.

Take a moment to think about how you worked the seed stitch, remembering that a knit stitch looks like a "V" and a purl stitch looks like a bump. When working in seed stitch you do the opposite of what the stitch on the left needle looks like. If you see a bump right under the needle, then knit the stitch. Or, if you see a "V" under the needle, then purl the stitch.

✕ **TIP** *When making an item using seed stitch it's easier to cast on an odd number of stitches. That way every row begins and ends with a knit stitch.*

practice swatch

Seed Stitch

Practice seed stitch by making a practice swatch using worsted weight yarn and US size 8 (5 mm) 9" (23 cm) single-pointed needles.

Cast on 21 stitches.

1 **Row 1:** K1, move yarn to front of needle, *p1, move yarn to back of needle, k1, move yarn to front of needle*; repeat from * to * to end of row.

Continue repeating row 1 until you are completely comfortable with the seed stitch. Bind off in pattern following the directions on page 55.

knit this stitch
purl this stitch

RIBBING

In ribbing, the same stitches line up in vertical columns, knit stitches directly above knit stitches and purl stitches directly above purl stitches. You won't use ribbing until later in the book but it's taught here because of its close resemblance to seed stitch. Ribbing is frequently used in knitting. It has a great deal of elasticity, which allows it to contract, making it an ideal stitch for waistlines and cuffs on sweaters or the brim of a hat. In order to make it fit more closely, ribbing is often worked on smaller needles than those used for the body of the garment. Sometimes ribbing is referred to as 2 × 2 or 3 × 3, etc. These numbers specify the distribution of knits and purls in each ribbing repeat. In other words, 2 × 2 would be a knit 2, purl 2 ribbing.

For ribbing, you always work the stitch in the same manner it presents itself. If you see the "V" of a knit stitch, then work the new stitch in knit; if you see the bump of a purl, then work the new stitch in purl.

Do not steam block ribbing. Once steam blocked, ribbing will remain stretched out. The photo at right shows a swatch that has been steam blocked open so that the details can be seen.

BINDING OFF IN PATTERN

Sometimes when you have made an item that has a pattern stitch such as ribbing or seed stitch all the way to the edge, the directions might call for binding off in pattern. This just means that you should maintain the same pattern stitch (for instance *k1, p1*) in the bind-off row as was used in the preceding rows. Maintain the knit or purl pattern as specified by the directions but work the bind-off on the right needle, continuing to pass the first stitch over the second stitch on the right needle.

practice swatch
Ribbing

Learn more about the different types of ribbing by making a practice swatch using worsted weight yarn and US size 8 (5 mm) 9" (23 cm) single-pointed needles.

Cast on 24 stitches. Learn how to knit a variety of rib stitches by working the following rows:

Rows 1 to 8 (1 x 1 rib): *K1, p1*; repeat from * to * to end of row.

Rows 9 to 16 (2 x 2 rib): *K2, p2*; repeat from * to * to end of row.

Rows 17 to 24 (3 x 3 rib): *K3, p3*; repeat from * to * to end of row.

Rows 25 to 36 (4 x 4 rib): *K4, p4*; repeat from * to * to end of row.

Bind off in pattern.

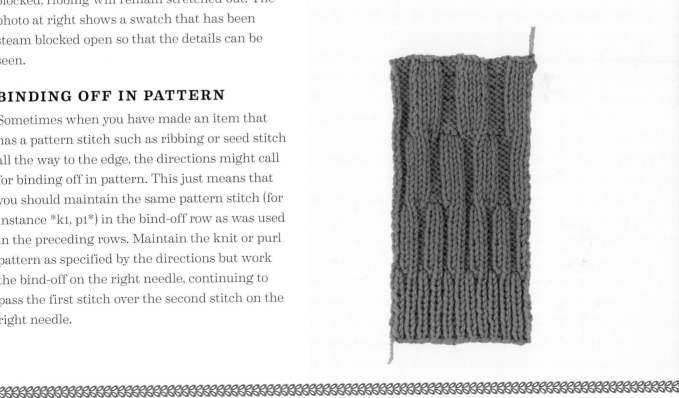

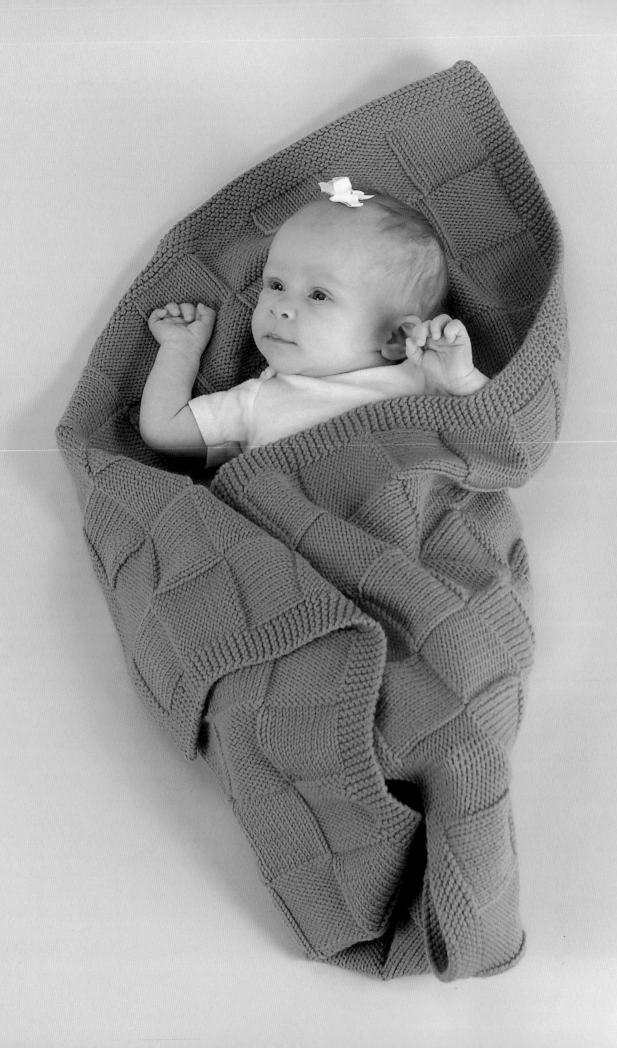

BABY BLOCKS BLANKET

A baby blanket made with blocks of stockinette stitch and reverse stockinette stitch is a great project for you to learn and practice a new skill: purling. The blanket is a perfect size for baby to bring along in a car seat or stroller.

MATERIALS

YARN

○  medium weight smooth yarn, approx. 715 yd (654 m). Since this is a baby blanket, consider using a yarn that is washable, such as a wool and acrylic blend or washable wool.

NEEDLES AND NOTIONS

○ US size 7 (4.5 mm) circular needle at least 24" (61 cm) long or size needed to achieve gauge. The circular needle is necessary to accommodate the large number of stitches. You will be knitting back and forth on the circular needle.

○ yarn needle for weaving in ends

○ stitch markers

○ rust-proof pins for blocking

EQUIPMENT

○ washing machine

○ towels

GAUGE

○ 20 sts = 4" (10 cm) in stockinette stitch

FINISHED DIMENSIONS

○ 28½" (72 cm) by 28½" (72 cm)

SKILLS

○ purling

○ cable cast-on

○ using a circular needle to knit back and forth

○ using stitch markers

○ modifying a pattern to make the item bigger or smaller

○ alternating between knit and purl in the same row

○ reading a stitch pattern with repeats

○ combining garter stitch, stockinette stitch, and reverse stockinette stitch in a block pattern

○ damp blocking

HOW TO KNIT THE BABY BLOCKS BLANKET

1 Cast on stitches and make blanket edging placing markers on final row of edging.

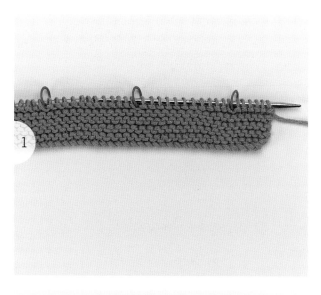

Cast on 144 sts using the cable cast-on method.

Rows 1 to 10: Knit.

Row 11: K6, [pm, k12] repeat 11 times, pm, k6.

2 Make first set of blocks.

Row 1: K6, [sm, k12, p12] 5 times, sm, k12, sm, k6.

Row 2: K6, [sm, p12, k12] 5 times, sm, p12, sm, k6.

Rows 3 to 18: Repeat rows 1 and 2 eight more times.

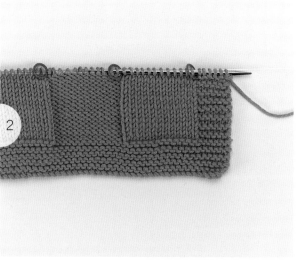

3 Make second set of blocks.

Row 19: K6, [sm, p12, k12] 5 times, sm, p12, sm, k6.

Row 20: K6, [sm, k12, p12] 5 times, sm, k12, sm, k6.

Rows 21 to 36: Repeat rows 19 and 20 eight more times.

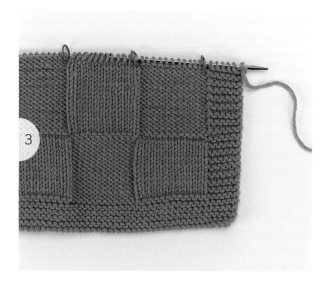

4 Continue knitting until 11 sets of blocks are completed. You can now see how the two groups of 18 rows (36 rows total) form two sets of blocks made from contrasting stockinette stitch and reverse stockinet stitch. The 36-row repeat is worked four more times and then the first 18 rows are repeated once.

Rows 37 to 180: Repeat rows 1 to 36 four more times.

Rows 181 to 198: Repeat rows 1 to 18 once.

5 Remove stitch markers and make edging.

Row 1: Knit, removing stitch markers as you come to them.

Rows 2 to 11: Knit.

6 Bind off loosely and evenly. Cut yarn, leaving a tail at least 8" (20 cm) long.

7 Finishing: weave in all ends and damp block if desired.

MODIFYING THE PATTERN TO BE BIGGER OR SMALLER

A stitch pattern is a multiple of a given number of stitches. That is true of the blocks pattern used to make this blanket. Each block is 12 stitches wide and there are eleven blocks (132 stitches). In addition, there are 6 edge stitches (worked in garter stitch – all knit) on either side, an additional 12 stitches for a total of 144 stitches in the pattern. As you can see, this pattern is a multiple of 12 stitches. If you want to make the blanket wider, then add stitches in a multiple of 12; likewise if you want it to be narrower, then subtract stitches in a multiple of 12. For instance, if you want to add two extra blocks to the width (2 × 12), then you would cast on 168 stitches (144 + 24).

In addition to a pattern repeat worked into the number of stitches, a pattern usually has a row repeat as well. This pattern is worked for 18 rows, at which point the stockinette stitch and reverse stockinette stitch sections are switched for another 18 rows. So, the pattern has a 36-row repeat for two complete sets of alternating blocks. However if you only want to add one additional set of blocks you would add a single set of 18 rows.

SEED STITCH TABLE RUNNER

Seed stitch is one of the most useful and versatile stitches available to knitters. The edges don't curl, making it a perfect stitch for scarves and blankets. The rhythmic repetition of the bumps is ideal for accentuating variegated yarns, but it adds interest to solid-colored pieces as well. Seed stitch also drapes beautifully. Seed stitch works well when using needles larger than is typical for the weight of yarn, making it an excellent way to get more knit area from less yarn and allowing you to use a yarn that you might otherwise think twice about buying because of its price but can't resist because of its beauty.

MATERIALS

YARN

○ (6) super bulky weight smooth, variegated yarn, approx. 200 yd (183 m)

NEEDLES AND NOTIONS

○ US size 13 (9 mm) 9" (23 cm) single-pointed needles or size needed to achieve gauge

○ yarn needle for weaving in ends

GAUGE

○ 10 sts = 4" (10 cm) in seed stitch

FINISHED DIMENSIONS

○ 11½" x 38"(29 x 97 cm)

SKILLS

○ knit seed stitch

○ knit ribbing

○ bind off stitches in pattern

○ English and Continental methods of knitting

HOW TO KNIT THE SEED STITCH TABLE RUNNER

1 Cast on 29 stitches.

2 **Row 1:** *K1, p1*; repeat from * to * to end of row.

Repeat row 1 until the length from the cast-on edge is approximately 38" (97 cm) or the desired length. Be sure to leave at least 2 yds (1.8 m) for binding off.

3 Bind off stitches in pattern as follows:

Step 1: K1.

Step 2: P1.

Step 3: Pass first stitch on right needle over second stitch and off the end of the needle (one stitch has been bound off).

Step 4: K1.

Step 5: Pass first stitch on right needle over second stitch and off the end of the needle (one stitch has been bound off).

Repeat bind off steps 2 to 5 until 1 stitch remains on needle. Cut yarn leaving a tail at least 8" (20 cm) long and pull through last stitch, tighten to secure.

4 To finish, weave in ends. Damp block or steam block if the yarn you've chosen does not contain acrylic or nylon. See page 50 for more information on steam blocking.

MODIFYING THE PATTERN
TO MAKE A SCARF

This design can easily be modified to make a scarf by casting on fewer stitches and making a narrower but longer piece. Seed stitch is easiest to knit with an odd number of stitches so that you don't need to remember whether you're on the right side or wrong side. If you work seed stitch with an odd number of stitches, then every row is worked identically.

To make a scarf instead, cast on 17 stitches. Follow the stitch pattern until there is just enough yarn to bind off or until you have reached the desired length. If you use the same amount of yarn as the table runner and you knit at the same gauge, you should get a scarf that is about 6¾" (17 cm) by 65" (165 cm).

SHAPING

One of the reasons knitting is so versatile is that it's easy to shape an item by either increasing or decreasing the number of stitches. In this section you will learn different methods for increasing and decreasing, the effect and appearance of each method, and which methods to use for different situations.

skills and useful information

INCREASES AND DECREASES

A very simple increase can be accomplished by knitting into the same stitch twice, thereby adding 1 stitch (knit front and back—kf&b). By knitting 2 stitches together at the same time (knit 2 together—k2tog) the number of stitches can be decreased by 1. There are actually many ways to increase and decrease in knitting, and each method results in a different look. The primary distinction is the direction in which the stitches slant—either to the right or to the left—after the increase or decrease. For example, the direction of the stitch slant is important if you are making the neck opening in a V-neck sweater. The stitches on the right side of the "V" should point to the right and the stitches on the left side of the "V" should point to the left.

Before starting the project in this chapter there are some basic increases and decreases to be learned. Master all of the shaping techniques on the practice swatch before you jump into the project.

INCREASES
Knit Front and Back (kf&b)

This is the most simple and easily learned increase. It is often referred to as the bar increase because a small bar is formed on the right side of the knitting.

1 First knit in the usual way but don't take the new stitch off your needle.

2 Pivot the right needle to the back of the left needle and insert it knitwise (from front to back) into the back loop of the same stitch just worked.

3 Make another stitch into the back loop and pull the new loop through to the front of the knitting.

4 Slip the old stitch off the left needle along with the 2 stitches just made on the right needle. There are now 2 stitches in place of 1.

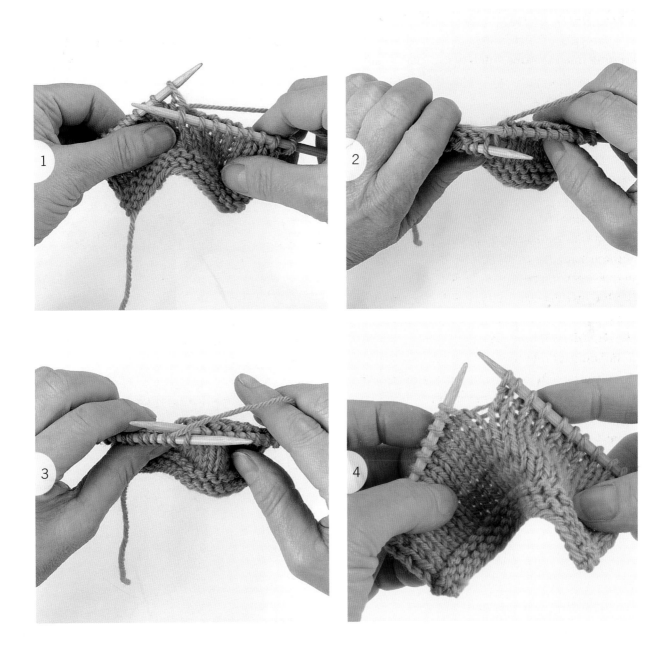

Purl Front and Back (pf&b)

1 First purl in the usual way but don't take the new stitch off the needle.

2 Keeping the working yarn in front, pivot the right needle to the back of the left needle.

3 Insert right needle purlwise (from back to front) into the back loop of the same stitch just worked.

4 Now make another purl stitch in the back loop.

5 Pull the new loop to the back of the knitting. Slip the old stitch off the left needle along with the 2 stitches just made on the right needle. There are now 2 stitches in place of 1.

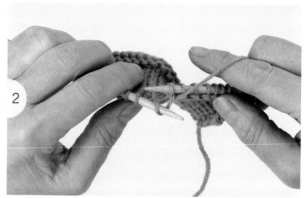

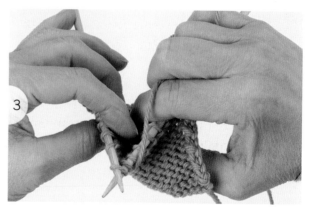

MAKE ONE (M1)

The make one (M1) increases can slant to either the right or the left, but both increases have in common the fact that they make a stitch out of the horizontal bar or "ladder" that extends between every 2 stitches. The horizontal bar is picked up onto the left needle and then worked as a knit stitch. When working the new stitch the bar is given a twist to avoid a large hole in the knitting. The directional slant of the increase is caused by how the bar is picked up, either from the front or the back. This increase is sometimes referred to as a lifted increase.

Make One Right (M1R)—slants to the right

1 Working from back to front, insert left needle under the horizontal bar between the stitch on the right needle and the stitch on the left needle.

2 Insert right needle from the left (**A**) to the right (**B**) under the strand on the front of the left needle, thereby twisting it and preventing a hole.

3 Wrap the yarn around the right needle to form a new stitch and slip the new stitch and the picked-up strand off the left needle. One new stitch has been added.

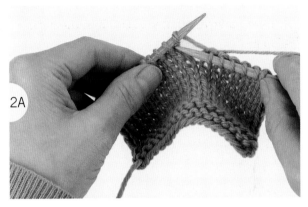

Make One Left (M1L)—slants to the left

1 Working from front to back, insert left needle under the horizontal bar between the stitch on the right needle and the stitch on the left needle.

2 Insert the right needle from the right to the left under the strand on the back of the left needle thereby twisting it and preventing a hole.

3 Wrap the yarn around the right needle to form a new stitch and slip the new stitch and the picked-up strand off the left needle. One new stitch has been added.

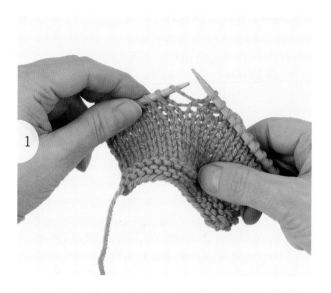

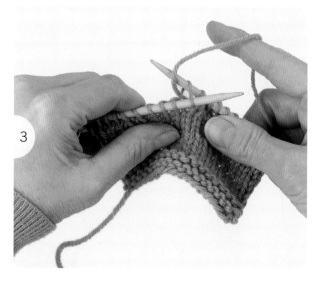

YARNOVER (YO)

A yarnover is a very fast increase to work but keep in mind that it leaves a visible hole in your knitting.

1 Bring yarn forward between needles.

2 Lay the yarn over the right needle in a counterclockwise direction ending behind the needle. One new stitch has been added.

3 Knit the next stitch. Notice that the yarnover has made an extra loop on the right needle that is worked as a stitch on the next row. The yarnover loop can be worked as a knit stitch or purl stitch (shown).

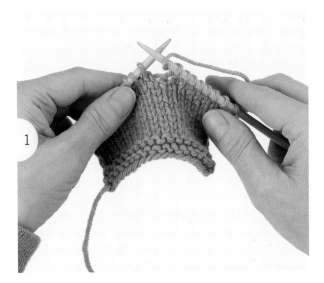

practice swatch

Increasing

Practice increasing stitches by making a swatch using worsted weight yarn and US size 8 (5 mm) 9" (23 cm) single-pointed needles. As you practice the increases, notice how the stitches slant to the right or the left. Increases and decreases are rarely worked on the edge stitch; rather, one or more plain stitches is made first.

After each section of the swatch is completed feel free to repeat the section several more times for more practice. Notice that 2 plain stitches are worked at both the beginning and the end of the row and followed or preceded by the increase. The stitches in the middle are worked even (without increasing or decreasing) in either purl on the wrong side or knit on the right side.

Cast on 8 sts.

Knit Front and Back (kf&b)

Row 1 (WS): Purl.

Row 2 (RS): K2, kf&b, k2, kf&b, k2—10 sts.

Row 3: Purl.

Row 4: K2, kf&b, k4, kf&b, k2—12 sts.

Row 5: Purl.

Row 6: K2, kf&b, k6, kf&b, k2—14 sts.

Row 7: Purl.

Purl Front and Back (pf&b)

Row 8: Knit.

Row 9: P2, pf&b, p8, pf&b, p2—16 sts.

Row 10: Knit.

Row 11: P2, pf&b, p10, pf&b, p2—18 sts.

Row 12: Knit.

Row 13: P2, pf&b, p12, pf&b, p2—18 sts.

Row 14: Knit.

Yarnover (yo)

Row 15: Purl.

Row 16: K2, yo, k14, yo, k2—20 sts.

Row 17: Purl.

Row 18: K2, yo, k16, yo, k2—22 sts.

Row 19: Purl.

Row 20: K2, yo, k18, yo, k2—24 sts.

Row 21: Purl.

Make One Right (M1R)

and Make One Left (M1L)

Row 22: K2, M1R, k20, M1L, k2—26 sts.

Row 23: Purl.

Row 24: K2, M1R, k22, M1L, k2—28 sts.

Row 29: Purl.

Row 30: K2, M1R, k24, M1L, k2—30 sts.

Row 31: Purl.

Continue practicing until you feel comfortable with the increases. Don't bind off the swatch; save if for practicing the decreases. Take a moment to observe the different appearance of the increases.

DECREASES

All decreases are accomplished by working 2 stitches together at the same time. The slant is created by working either through the front of the loops or the back of the loops.

Knit Two Together (k2tog)— slants to the right

This is the easiest decrease to make and is easily remembered.

1 Insert the right needle knitwise into the next 2 stitches on the left needle.

2 Wrap the yarn around the right needle.

3 Knit these 2 stitches at the same time as if they were 1 stitch. There is now 1 stitch in the place of 2 stitches.

Purl Two Together (p2tog)— slants to the right on the knit side

This is very similar to the k2tog but rarely used (you'll see it in the directions for the knit bobbles).

1 Insert the right needle purlwise into the next 2 stitches on the left needle. Wrap the yarn around the needle and purl these 2 stitches at the same time as if they were 1 stitch. There is now 1 stitch in the place of 2.

Slip, Slip, Knit (ssk)—slants to the left

1 This decrease is very similar to the k2tog except that the decrease is worked through the back loops of 2 stitches at a time. Working one at a time, slip the next 2 stitches knitwise to right needle.

2 Insert the tip of the left needle into the front loops of these 2 stitches.

3 Knit these stitches at the same time through the back loops as if they were 1 stitch.

practice swatch

Decreasing

Continue working on the practice swatch from increasing (page 72) to learn the decreases.

Row 32: K2, ssk, K22, k2tog, k2—28 sts remain.
Row 33: Purl.
Row 34: K2, ssk, K20, k2tog, k2—26 sts remain.
Row 35: Purl.
Row 36: K2, ssk, K18, k2tog, k2—24 sts remain.
Row 37: Purl.
Row 38: K2, ssk, K16, k2tog, k2—22 sts remain.
Row 39: Purl.
Row 40: K2, ssk, K14, k2tog, k2—20 sts remain.
Row 41: Purl.
Row 42: K2, ssk, K12, k2tog, k2—18 sts remain.

Bind off all stitches now or continue practicing as you desire. Take a moment to observe the different appearances of the decreases.

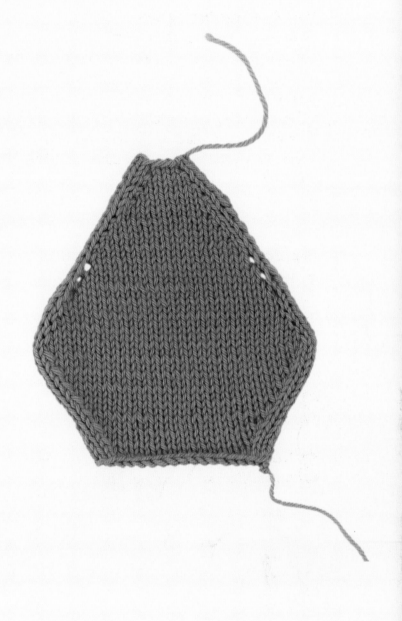

LEAF EDGE SHAWL

This lovely shawl has a treasure trove of increases and decreases. The basic triangular shape in the center is formed by increasing on each edge of the triangle on every other row. The leaf design is shaped using right and left slanting increases and decreases. The eyelet edging is created using a yarnover increase paired with a decrease. It sounds complicated here but once you follow the step-by-step directions you'll see how simple it really is to use increases and decreases to shape your knitting and add visual appeal.

Since this is meant to be a cozy shawl, be sure the yarn is soft. Wool is a great choice for warmth, but if you can find a wool and silk blend or a wool and bamboo blend the shawl will have a better drape.

MATERIALS

YARN

-  medium weight smooth yarn, approx. 625 yd (572 m)

NEEDLES AND NOTIONS

- US size 7 (4.5 mm) 29" (74 cm) circular needle or size needed to achieve gauge
- US size 9 (5.5 mm) straight or circular needle at least two sizes bigger than smaller needle for binding off only
- yarn needle for weaving in ends
- rust-proof pins for blocking

EQUIPMENT

- iron
- ironing board

GAUGE

- 18 sts = 4" (10 cm) in stockinette stitch

FINISHED DIMENSIONS

- 53" (135 cm) at widest point x 26" (66 cm) depth

SKILLS

- increase the number of stitches using the following techniques:

  knit front and back (kf&b)
  yarnover (yo)
  make one left (M1R)
  make one right (M1L)

- decrease the number of stitches using the following techniques:

  knit two together (k2tog)
  slip, slip, knit (ssk)

HOW TO KNIT THE SHAWL

1 To begin, you will cast on stitches and work a few increase rows to establish the basic triangle shape. Use the smaller sized circular needle. At the end of each row, you will find stated the number of stitches you should have after completing the row. It's a good idea to count your stitches and make sure your count is the same as the directions. See the note about working back and forth on a circular needle on page 48.

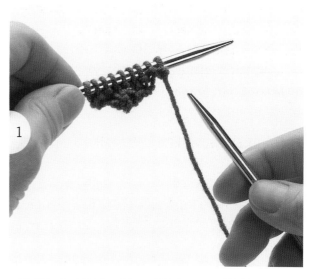

Cast on 3 sts.
Row 1: Kf&b, k1, kf&b—5 sts.
Row 2: Kf&b, k3, kf&b—7 sts.
Row 3: Kf&b, k1, p1, k1, p1, k1, kf&b—9 sts.

2 Make one increases (M1) are used on either side of the three center stitches to widen the leaves. It can be difficult on these beginningrows to find the bar used to work the increase. Firmly stretch the stitches between the right and left needle to find the bar. Also, beginning on row 4, you will start the eyelet edging that is made with the first and last 3 stitches of the row.

Row 4: K1, yo, k2tog, M1R, k3, M1L, ssk, yo, k1—11 sts.
Row 5: K3, p2, k1, p2, k3.
Row 6: K1, yo, k2tog, k1, M1R, k3, M1L, k1, ssk, yo, k1—13 sts.
Row 7: K3, p3, k1, p3, k3.
Row 8: K1, yo, k2tog, k2, M1R, k3, M1L, k2, ssk, yo, k1—15 sts.
Row 9: K3, p4, k1, p4, k3.

3 Mark the right side (RS) of the shawl with an open stitch marker or a safety pin now (sufficient rows have been worked to allow the space). The right-side rows are even numbered, and they are also the rows in which all the increases and decreases are made.

Row 10 (RS): K1, yo, k2tog, k3, M1R, k3, M1L, k3, ssk, yo, k1—17 sts.
Row 11: K3, p5, k1, p5, k3.
Row 12: K1, yo, k2tog, k4, M1R, k3, M1L, k4, ssk, yo, k1—19 sts.

4 Stitch markers are added (pm—place marker) to delineate the center triangular section from this point forward. As your shawl progresses, more and more stitches will be added between the markers. When you reach a marker, slip it from the left needle to the right needle (sm—slip marker) and continue with the directions.

Row 13: K3, p6, pm, kf&b, pm, p6, k3—20 sts.

(continued)

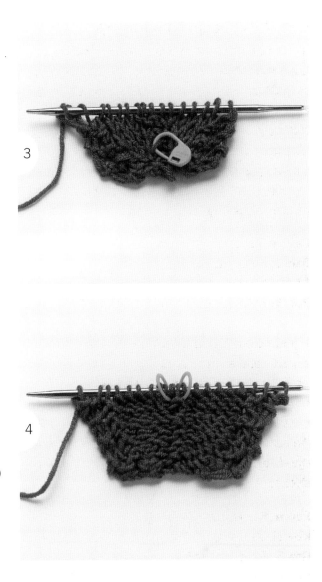

5 The increases for the leaf shape are complete and now decreases will be worked to taper the leaf to a single stitch. On right side rows (even numbered), a kf&b increase is worked to offset the decrease made to the leaf shape but the total number of stitches will not change on the row. For this section, the stitch count will increase on wrong side (odd-numbered) rows. So, on both right-side and wrong-side rows, a stitch adjacent to each marker will be worked with a kf&b increase. After completing the first 23 rows, you can see that the shawl is beginning to form a triangular shape and the first set of leaf edging stitches are complete.

5

Row 14: K1, yo, k2tog, ssk, k4, sm, kf&b, kf&b, sm, k4, k2tog, ssk, yo, k1.

Row 15: K3, p5, sm, kf&b, knit until 1 st remains before marker, kf&b, sm, p5, k3—22 sts.

Row 16: K1, yo, k2tog, ssk, k3, sm, kf&b, knit until 1 st remains before marker, kf&b, sm, k3, k2tog, ssk, yo, k1.

Row 17: K3, p4, sm, kf&b, knit until 1 st remains before marker, kf&b, sm, p4, k3—24 sts.

Row 18: K1, yo, k2tog, ssk, k2, sm, kf&b, knit until 1 st remains before marker, kf&b, sm, k2, k2tog, ssk, yo, k1.

Row 19: K3, p3, sm, kf&b, knit until 1 st remains before marker, kf&b, sm, p3, k3—26 sts.

Row 20: K1, yo, k2tog, ssk, k1, sm, kf&b, knit until 1 st remains before marker, kf&b, sm, k1, k2tog, ssk, yo, k1.

Row 21: K3, p2, sm, kf&b, knit until 1 st remains before marker, kf&b, sm, p2, k3—28 sts.

Row 22: K1, yo, k2tog, ssk, sm, kf&b, knit until 1 st remains before marker, kf&b, sm, k2tog, ssk, yo, k1.

Row 23: K3, p1, sm, kf&b, knit until 1 st remains before marker, kf&b, sm, p1, k3—30 sts.

The next 20 rows will establish the basic directions that will be repeated over and over until the shawl reaches the desired width and is ready to be finished off on the top (or widest) edge. From this point forward, the stitch count will not be shown at the end of the row. Instead you will be given a reminder at the end of the rows in which the total stitch count increases. Just remember that the stitch count will increase by two on every right side (even-numbered) row as the leaf shape gets wider. As the leaf is being tapered down to 1 stitch, the stitch count will increase on every wrong-side (odd-numbered) row. This is where the pin that you used to mark the right side rows will come in handy. Every 20-row repeat of the basic directions will increase the total stitch count by 20 stitches. The picture below shows the shawl after completion of row 43.

Row 24: K1, yo, k2tog, M1R, k1, sm, knit to next marker, sm, k1, M1L, ssk, yo, k1—2 sts increased.
Row 25: K3, p2, sm, knit to next marker, sm, p2, k3.
Row 26: K1, yo, k2tog, k1, M1R, k1, sm, knit to next marker, sm, k1, M1L, k1, ssk, yo, k1—2 sts increased.
Row 27: K3, p3, sm, knit to next marker, sm, p3, k3.
Row 28: K1, yo, k2tog, k2, M1R, k1, sm, knit to next marker, sm, k1, M1L, k2, ssk, yo, k1—2 sts increased.
Row 29: K3, p4, sm, knit to next marker, sm, p4, k3.
Row 30: K1, yo, k2tog, k3, M1R, k1, sm, knit to next marker, sm, k1, M1L, k3, ssk, yo, k1—2 sts increased.
Row 31: K3, p5, sm, knit to next marker, sm, p5, k3.
Row 32: K1, yo, k2tog, k4, M1R, k1, sm, knit to next marker, sm, k1, M1L, k4, ssk, yo, k1—2 sts increased.
Row 33: K3, p6, sm, knit to next marker, sm, p6, k3.

6

Row 34: K1, yo, k2tog, ssk, k4, sm, knit to next marker, sm, k4, k2tog, ssk, yo, k1.
Row 35: K3, p5, sm, kf&b, knit until 1 st remains before marker, kf&b, sm, p5, k3—2 sts increased.
Row 36: K1, yo, k2tog, ssk, k3, sm, kf&b, knit until 1 st remains before marker, kf&b, sm, k3, k2tog, ssk, yo, k1.
Row 37: K3, p4, sm, kf&b, knit until 1 st remains before marker, kf&b, sm, p4, k3—2 sts increased.
Row 38: K1, yo, k2tog, ssk, k2, sm, kf&b, knit until 1 st remains before marker, kf&b, sm, k2, k2tog, ssk, yo, k1.
Row 39: K3, p3, sm, kf&b, knit until 1 st remains before marker, kf&b, sm, p3, k3—2 sts increased.
Row 40: K1, yo, k2tog, ssk, k1, sm, kf&b, knit until 1 st remains before marker, kf&b, sm, k1, k2tog, ssk, yo, k1.
Row 41: K3, p2, sm, kf&b, knit until 1 st remains before marker, kf&b, sm, p2, k3—2 sts increased.
Row 42: K1, yo, k2tog, ssk, sm, kf&b, knit until 1 st remains before marker, kf&b, sm, k2tog, ssk, yo, k1.
Row 43: K3, p1, sm, kf&b, knit until 1 st remains before marker, kf&b, sm, p1, k3—2 sts increased.

(continued)

7 Repeat rows 24 to 43 (a total of 20 rows) over and over until 11 leaf shapes have been completed (223 rows in total). You can make the shawl smaller or bigger by changing the number of times rows 24 to 43 are repeated. For a smaller shawl, complete fewer repeats; for a larger shawl, add a few repeats more. If you follow the directions exactly, completing a total of 11 leaf shapes, then the total stitch count will be 230 stitches. Shown at right is the shawl after the completion of the beginning 23 rows plus three repeats of the 20-row leaf sequence.

7

8 Once the desired number of rows have been completed for the body of the shawl, three additional rows are worked to finish the top edge. The edging rows should only be worked after the completion of a row 41; the wrong-side (odd-numbered) row that is made after the leaf shape has been tapered to 1 stitch. The stitch count will increase by one on the first edge row but after that will remain the same. It is very important that the top edge be bound off loosely; if it's too tight then the edge will curl. To bind off loosely, use a larger needle for just the right-hand needle when binding off. Since the right-hand needle will only have 2 stitches at any time in does not need to be a circular needle; a straight needle works just as well.

8

Row 1 (RS): K1, *yo, k2tog*; repeat from * to * until 1 st remains, yo, k1—1 st increased.
Row 2: Purl all sts.
Row 3: Knit all sts.

Bind off all stitches loosely and evenly using a needle two sizes bigger than the needle used to knit the shawl. Using the yarn needle, weave in all ends.

HOW TO FINISH THE SHAWL

9 After the knitting is finished, you will find that the leaf edging tends to curl under. This is remedied by steaming the edge using a steam iron. At no point should the steam iron actually touch the knitting. Hold the iron 1" (2.5cm) above. Lay the shawl on your ironing board and, working in sections, hold the iron above the shawl and allow the steam to penetrate the shawl.

9

10 Set the iron aside. Using your hands, gently stretch and smooth the leaf shape until it lies flat.

10

11 Once all the edges have been steamed, lay the shawl on a blocking board or carpeted floor and pin all three edges, placing a pin about every 5" (13 cm). The top edge should be pinned so that it is straight and even. The leaf edges are fluted so don't try to straighten the edge; rather, make sure the leaves lie flat and the triangle shape is consistent from side to side.

11

12 Cover the entire shawl with a towel that is just barely wet (wet the towel in the washer and then spin it dry). If necessary, use more than one towel. Leave the towel in place for at least four hours; it can actually be left on the shawl until it's completely dry. Once blocking is finished, your shawl is ready to wear.

HOW TO CARE FOR THE SHAWL

The center of the portion of the shawl is worked in garter stitch, which has a tendency to stretch. Your shawl should not be stored hanging. Instead, fold it and keep it on a shelf.

12

KNITTING IN THE ROUND

One of the knitting world's most handy tools is the circular needle, which is two short needles that are connected with a cable. You've already learned how to use a circular needle to knit a project that has too many stitches to fit on a single-pointed needle. In this section, you'll learn how to use a circular needle to make a cylindrical item. In addition, you will find information for knitting with double-pointed needles to shape the crown of a hat and as a substitute for circular needles.

skills and useful information

CIRCULAR NEEDLES

Circular needles come in a variety of lengths (measured from needle tip to needle tip). When used for knitting in the round, the length of the needle when joined from tip to tip will equal the circumference of the circle. Circular needles are used for knitting in the round (making a cylinder) as well as for knitting back and forth on a flat item with many stitches.

LENGTH	COMMON USES
16" (41 cm)	Hats, small bags
24" (61 cm)	Children's sweaters, tote bags
29" (74 cm)	Children's and small adults' sweaters
32" (81 cm)	Children's and small adults' sweaters
40" (101.5 cm)	Medium and large adults' sweaters

How to Knit in the Round on a Circular Needle

Using a circular needle to knit in the round is quite simple except that it is important that the stitches not be twisted when the circle is first made. Every pattern for knitting in the round will say something like "Join in the round being careful not to twist". You will learn in the practice swatch below how to join in the round without twisting the stitches.

The common needle lengths for knitting in the round are shown in the chart to the left. You can find shorter and longer lengths not listed on the chart, but most patterns use lengths shown.

A circular needle can be used to make an item that is slightly larger than its circumference, but it cannot be used to make an item that is smaller than its circumference. More stitches can be squeezed together but there's a limit to how far apart the stitches can be stretched.

Stockinette Stitch in the Round Compared to Working Back and Forth on a Flat Item

Recall for a moment the beginning chapters of this book when you learned to make a flat item in stockinette stitch by alternating knit rows with purl rows. Think of what you learned this way: when knitting a flat item, the right side, the public side, is worked in knit stitch and the wrong side, the private side, is work in purl stitch. Because you are knitting back and forth, half of the rows are made using the knit stitch on the outside (the public side) and half of the rows are made using the purl stitch on the inside (the private side). However, when knitting in the round, for instance on a hat, you are always working on the outside (the public side). To make stockinette stitch in the round, every round is worked in knit stitch.

One interesting fact to note is that when knitting in the round, garter stitch is the opposite of stockinette stitch. Instead of knitting every row when working back and forth on a flat item, knit rows must be alternated with purl rows to execute garter stitch in the round.

practice swatch

Knitting in the Round on a Circular Needle

Learn how to knit in the round by making a practice swatch using worsted weight yarn and US size 8 (5 mm) 16" (41 cm) circular needle.

1 Cast on 80 stitches. You will find information about casting on to a circular needle in the Texture section, pg 48.

To avoid twisting the stitches, it is important that the chain of cast-on stitches does not spiral (or twist) around the needle. To avoid this problem, always make sure that the bumps at the bottom of the stitches are lined up facing the center of the circle formed by the needle. The stitches should be uniformly oriented as in the picture **(A)**.

The stitches in the picture below right **(B)** are spiraled or twisted around the needle. These stitches must be straightened before the knitting is joined in the round.

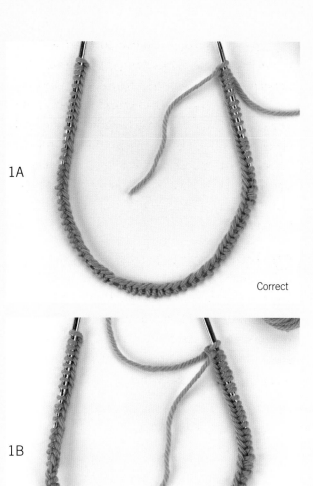

1A

Correct

1B

Incorrect

2 Line up the needles so that the last stitch
that was cast on is on the right along with the
working yarn. The first stitch that was cast on (the
slip knot) should be on the left. Before making the
first stitch, slip a circular stitch marker on the right
needle. Insert the right needle into the first stitch on
the left needle and use the working yarn to make a
stitch. Pull the working yarn firmly on this first stitch
to avoid a gap where the knitting is joined together in
the round.

3 Continue knitting around all the stitches on the
circular needle until you reach the stitch marker.
The marker indicates the beginning of the round
(BOR) and it should be slipped to the right needle
before each subsequent round. Every time you work
around the stitches and back to the BOR marker, 1
round has been completed.

2

3

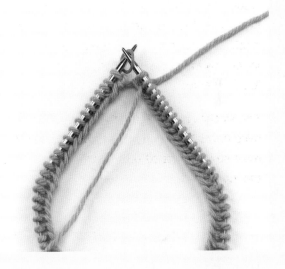

USING DOUBLE-POINTED NEEDLES TO SHAPE THE CROWN OF A HAT

A knit hat is started on circular needles using the same guidelines as shown on page 88. The first section of knitting used to make a hat is simply a cylinder with a height of anywhere from 5" (13 cm) to 8" (20 cm) or more depending on the size of the hat. Once the cylinder is completed then the crown must be shaped, somewhat like the top of a dome.

The shaping is accomplished by dividing the stitches into wedges that are gradually decreased to form a tapered top. As the stitches are decreased to form the tapered shape, the circumference of the cylinder will become smaller and no longer fit around the circular needle. At that point the stitches must be transferred to double-pointed needles to finish the remainder of the crown. Before you transfer the stitches to the double-pointed needles you will already have established the wedges marked by a line of decreases (k2tog).

1 Continuing in the same stitch pattern, knit the stitches off the circular needle and onto four double-pointed needles. Transfer the stitches on one of the plain knit rounds in between the decrease rounds.

2 The most effective arrangement of the stitches is to put two wedges onto each needle. Divide the stitches evenly into quarters with one of the k2tog decreases at the end of each needle. It's best to place the beginning-of-round (BOR) marker in the middle of one of the needles, so start to transfer the stitches at the beginning of the last wedge before the BOR marker.

3 Once all the stitches have been transferred to the double-pointed needles, use the fifth needle for knitting the stitches one needle at a time. Knit all the stitches from the first needle onto the free needle. When that needle is empty it becomes the new free needle and is used to knit the stitches on the next needle and so on around the hat.

4 After working through the decreases you will reach the point where just 8 stitches are left, 2 on each needle. Cut the working yarn leaving a tail at least 8" (20 cm) long and thread it on a yarn needle. Working in same order as used with knitting, thread the tail through each of the stitch loops around the top of the hat.

5 Pass the needle through the hole on the top of the hat to the inside, and pull it firmly to close the hole in the top of the hat. Weave the ends into the stitches on the inside of the hat to secure the ends.

USING DOUBLE-POINTED NEEDLES

Projects with a small circumference, such as socks or gold club covers are knit entirely with double-pointed needles. As a new knitter, avoid metal double-pointed needles; they are much too slippery. Use bamboo or wood instead. Also, don't use the very short double-pointed needles. Your needles should be at least 7" (18 cm).

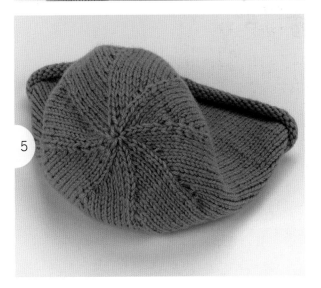

practice swatch

Knitting in the Round with Double-Pointed Needles

Learn how to use double-pointed needles to knit in the round by making a practice swatch using worsted weight yarn and a set of US size 8 (5 mm) 7" (18 cm) double-pointed needles.

Double-pointed needles are sold in sets of four or five. The stitches are divided between three or four needles and the free needle is used to knit.

1 Cast on 24 stitches to one of the double-pointed needles. Your cast-on stitches, especially the slip knot, should not be too tight. Transfer the stitches to the other two needles so that there are 8 stitches on each needle.

2 Just as with knitting in the round on a circular needle, it is critically important to be certain the stitches are not twisted around the needles. Lay the needles down on a table in the shape of a triangle and make certain that the bumps at the bottom of the stitches line up facing the center of the triangle.

3 The triangle should be pointing up. The first stitch to be cast on (the slip knot) will be on the top left needle and the last stitch and the working yarn will be on the top right needle. For ease of understanding, the needles will be numbered 1 to 3. The top left needle is number 1, the bottom needle is number 2, and the top right needle is number 3. With the needles remaining on the table, insert the free needle into the first stitch on needle 1, the top left needle.

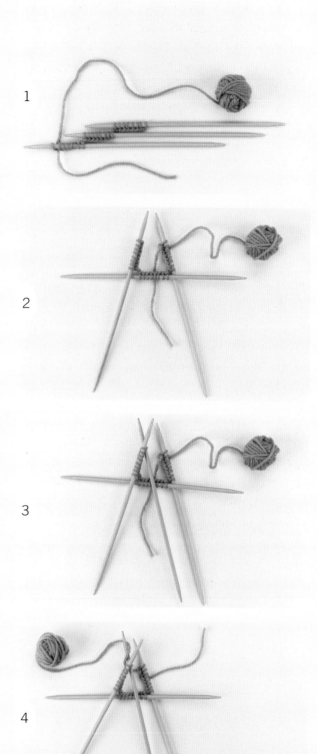

1

2

3

4

4 Use the working yarn coming from the last stitch cast on (needle 3) to make a loop around the free needle, then pull the loop through to make a new stitch. Pull the working yarn firmly on this first stitch to avoid a gap where the knitting is joined in the round. At this point, you can pick up the needles without fear of the stitches twisting.

5 Knit all the stitches from needle 1 onto the free needle.

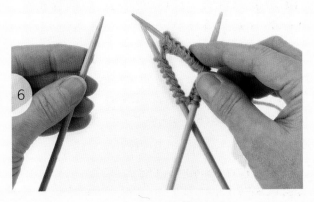

6 When needle 1 is empty it becomes the new free needle and is used to knit the stitches on the next needle (needle 2) and so on.

7 The best way to deal with the extra needles holding stitches waiting to be worked is to ignore them! Focus on the two needles being used at any time and hold them at the front of your work, allowing the unused needles to fall out of the way to the sides and back.

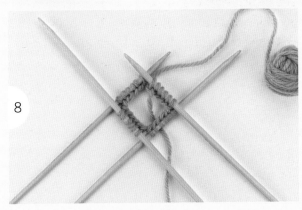

8 It is also possible to divide the stitches onto four needles instead of three. If choosing this arrangement then the needles are arranged into a square instead of a triangle. Use a locking stitch marker to indicate the beginning-of-round (BOR) stitch. Move the stitch marker up as you work.

EASY KNIT HAT

Making a simple hat is a terrific way to expand on the basic technique for knitting in the round. Once you get your stitches joined in the round you'll find this to be an easy, take-along project. Consider choosing an interesting yarn such as this self-striping yarn. Any small inconsistencies in your knitting will be disguised by the details in the yarn. The circumference of this hat is 20" (60 cm), which should fit most adults.

MATERIALS

YARN
○ **5** bulky weight, self-striping yarn, approx. 105 yd (96 m)

NEEDLES AND NOTIONS
○ US size 11 (8 mm) 16" (40 cm) circular needle or size needed to achieve gauge
○ US size 11 (8 mm) 7" (18 cm) double pointed needles or same size used to achieve gauge
○ circular stitch marker
○ yarn needle for weaving in ends

GAUGE

○ 12 sts = 4" (10 cm) in stockinette stitch

FINISHED DIMENSIONS

○ sized to fit a medium adult head
○ 20" (51 cm) circumference by 8" (20 cm) height

SKILLS

○ knitting a hat in the round using circular needles
○ changing to double-point needles from circular
○ adding a decorative braid to the top of the hat

HOW TO KNIT THE HAT

1. Cast on 60 stitches and join in the round being careful not to twist. Place marker to indicate the beginning of the round. Knit 2 rounds, slipping the marker as you come to it.

2. To stop the brim from rolling a few rounds of ribbing are added.

Round 1: *K2, p2*; repeat from * to * to end of round. Repeat round 1 three more times for a total of 4 ribbing rounds.

3. From this point on, knit all rounds. Continue knitting around and around until the length from the cast-on edge is approximately 5½" (13 cm). The rolled brim below the ribbing will need to be unrolled to obtain an accurate measurement.

4. Shape top. The stitches now need to be decreased to shape the crown. Work through all of the rows shown below. Change to double-pointed needles when the stitches will no longer fit comfortably around the circular needle. Use four double-pointed needles to hold the stitches and the fifth needle as the free needle for knitting. Arrange the stitches as shown in the Skills section (page 90) with 15 stitches on each needle to begin.

Round 2: *K13, k2tog*; repeat from * to * to end of round—56 sts remain.
Round 3: *K5, k2tog*; repeat from * to * to end of round—48 sts remain.
Round 4: Knit.
Round 5: *K4, k2tog*; repeat from * to * to end of round—40 sts remain.
Round 6: Knit.
Round 7: *K3, k2tog*; repeat from * to * to end of round—32 sts remain.
Round 8: Knit.
Round 9: *K2, k2tog*; repeat from * to * to end of round—24 sts remain.

Round 10: Knit.

Round 11: *K1, k2tog*; repeat from * to * to end of round—16 sts remain.

Round 12: Knit.

Round 13: *K2tog*; repeat from * to * to end of round—8 sts remain.

5 Finish the top. To finish the hat, cut the yarn, leaving a tail at least 8" (20 cm) long. Using a yarn needle, thread the tail through the remaining stitches and pass through the hole in the top of the hat to the inside. Pull the tail firmly to close the hole and weave the ends into the stitches in the inside of the hat to secure.

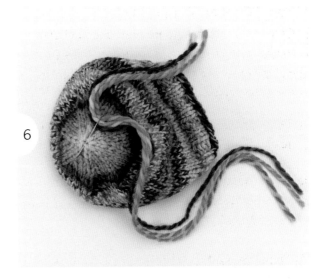

6 The last step is to add a decorative braid to the top. Begin by cutting three strands of yarn about 1 yd (0.9 m) long. Thread the strands onto the yarn needle and pass under a stitch on either side of the hole at the top of the hat. Pull the strands so that equal lengths are on either side of the center hole on top of the hat. There will now be six strands, three on either side of the hole.

7 Tie an overhand knot with all six of the strands. Divide the strands into two sections of three each and braid each section to the desired length. Tie an overhead knot at the end of the braid and trim the unused yarn.

8 Weave in all other ends and lightly steam block if desired.

PUTTING IT TOGETHER

By this point you've become a confident knitter who can make scarves, shawls, hats, and more. But what if you want to make something that is the combination of more than one piece? This chapter will teach you how to add a band of knitting to an existing item by picking up stitches. You'll also learn how join two pieces of knitting with a seam.

skills and useful information

PICK UP AND KNIT STITCHES

As your knitting progresses, you will often need to add a border or extra section to a piece of knitting that has already been finished. The stitches can be added on the bound-off edge or along the sides, such as a button band on a sweater. Borders and edges are normally worked in stitches that don't curl, such as ribbing, seed stitch, or garter stitch. For the directional block scarf (page 109), the technique is used to add the long bands to side of the center panel as well as the two short end bands.

You will most often hear this technique referred to as "pick up and knit stitches," but the words can be confusing. The stitch isn't actually knit as it's being picked up; rather, it is picked up knitwise onto the right needle to be knit (or purled) on the next row. Stitches are picked up with the right side of the work facing and using a separate ball of yarn.

2A

2B

1   When picking up stitches along a cast on or bound off edge, insert the right needle from the front to the back, going under two strands along the edge.

2   Wrap the yarn around the needle as if you were knitting and pull a loop through and onto the right needle (**2A**). You have picked up one stitch. Continue in this manner until the required number of stitches has been added (**2B**).

The number of stitches to be picked up varies depending on the edge from which you will be working. Typically, if stitches are being picked up from a cast-on or bound-off edge, then 1 stitch should be picked up for each stitch on the edge.

3

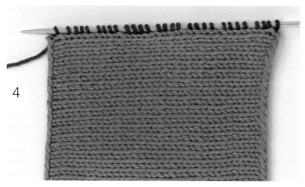

4

After the desired number of stitches have been picked up, then turn the work to the wrong side and continue with the directions (knit, rib, etc.).

3 When picking up stitches along a side edge (or selvedge edge) insert the needle into the space between the first and second stitch. Wrap the yarn around the needle as if you were knitting and pull a loop through onto the right needle.

4 If you are working along a side edge (or selvedge edge) of a scarf or sweater front, then you should not pick up a stitch for every row. Knit stitches are wider than they are tall, so stitches should be picked up in a ratio of about 3 stitches for every 4 rows or 5 stitches for every 7 rows. Don't worry about the space created by skipping a row; it won't be visible after the first row of knit or purl stitches is made. After the desired number of stitches have been picked up, then turn the work to the wrong side and continue with the directions (knit, rib, etc.).

WORKING WITH SELF-STRIPING YARN

Self striping yarn is dyed with intervals of changing colors that make stripes when knit. Because the intervals are fixed, for instance, 20 yards of one color connected to 20 yards of the next color, then the height of the stripe remains fairly consistent as long as the width of the knit object remains the same.

The scarf on page 109 has a narrow central panel with tall stripes composed of many rows of the same color. Attached to either side of the center panel are two strips that are knit the long way. Because this section is very wide (thirteen times more stitches than the center panel), it has very short stripes, sometimes 2 rows or less of a color. The schematic on page 110 shows the different sections of the scarf.

When working with self-striping yarn, it is important to remember that the number of stitches in the row will dictate the height of the stripe. If you make a cardigan sweater from self-striping yarn, then you can expect that the back, front, and sleeves will have stripes of differing heights because the width of each of those pieces is different. The scarf also combines stockinette stitch with garter stitch, and you'll notice how different self-striping yarn can look depending on the choice of stitch.

MAKING SEAMS— MATTRESS STITCH

Many knit garments require a seam of some sort; typically shoulders, sides, and sleeves are seamed. The quality of the seams and finishing on a garment are very important for its overall appeal. It's worth the time to learn how to seam neatly and securely. This is a skill that really must be practiced on swatches before sewing the seams on the garment you spent such a long time knitting.

Before seaming, the garment pieces should be blocked to make sure the size and shape match the pattern and also to make the sides smooth and even for easier seaming. In general, the same yarn that was used to knit the pieces should be used to make the seam. Exceptions would be highly textured or very thick yarn, in which case use a thinner yarn of the same fiber type in a matching color. The type of seam taught here is often referred to as the mattress stitch. It's a method of invisibly seaming by weaving the yarn back and forth between the two sides.

To aid in learning the technique use a contrasting yarn for making the practice seams, but remember that when you sew a garment together you want to use matching yarn. You should work on a flat table with adequate light and a comfortable chair.

USING A ROW COUNTER

The easiest way to make sure the pieces have exactly the same number or rows for seaming is to use a row counter. Keep track of the number of rows used to make the back using a row counter. When you make the two fronts, be certain they have the same number of rows as the back. You will have an area after the last decrease for the neck shaping to knit even (without increasing or decreasing) where you can adjust the row count to be equal to the back. Likewise, keep track of the number of rows completed to make the first sleeve and make certain the second sleeve matches.

practice swatch

Seams

To practice making seams, knit four practice swatches using worsted weight yarn and US size 8 (5 mm) 9" (23 cm) single-pointed needles. In the instructions that follow, you will seam the squares with rows running in different orientations, just as you might encounter in an actual garment. The methods vary slightly, so this is a good swatch to keep for reference whenever you need to sew seams.

Cast on 25 sts.
Row 1: Knit.
Row 2: Purl.
Repeat rows 1 and 2 for 26 rows and bind off.

STARTING THE SEAMING YARN

All three methods use the same technique to start the seaming yarn with a figure 8 between the two sides.

1 Cut a piece of contrasting yarn 24" (61 cm) long and thread it on a yarn needle. Insert the needle from back to front in the lower left corner of theright-hand piece.

2 Leave a tail at least 8" (20 cm) long to be wovenin. Form a figure 8 by passing the yarn from back to front in the lower right corner of the left-hand piece.

3 Next, pass the yarn from back to front through the same hole on the right-hand piece where you began.

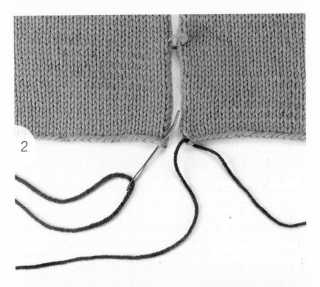

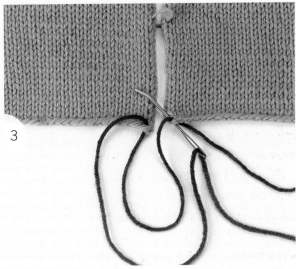

INVISIBLE SEAM FOR WEAVING THE VERTICAL (SIDE) EDGES OF STOCKINETTE STITCH

This type of seam is used to join side edges.

1 Align the swatches with the right sides facing up and two side edges abutting each other. Use safety pins or locking stitch markers to pin the pieces together and start the seaming yarn as shown on page 103.

2 You are going to be weaving back and forth between the pieces, working one stitch in from the side edge. If you pull the knitting crosswise you will see short horizontal bars between the edge stitch and the second stitch for each row of knitting.

3 Pass the threaded needle under two bars on the left side.

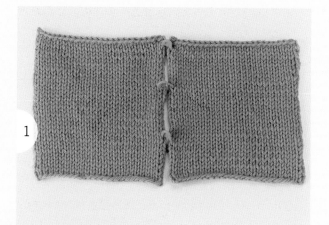

4 Next, pass the needle under two bars on the right side.

5 Inserting the needle into the same space from which it exited, continue alternating from side to side. Work upward without skipping any bars. Remove pins as you come to them. When pulling the yarn to tighten, pull in the same direction as the seam and keep the yarn parallel to the flat surface instead of pulling it toward you. At the end of the seam, pass the threaded needle to the wrong side and make a back stitch or two in the seam. Finish by weaving in the ends securely.

✗ **TIP** *If the two pieces you are seaming are not exactly symmetrical, you can compensate by passing the threaded needle under two bars on the longer piece and one bar on the shorter piece until the extra length is eased.*

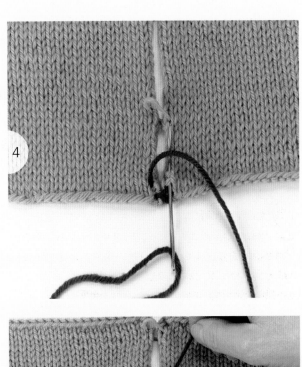

INVISIBLE SEAM FOR WEAVING THE HORIZONTAL (BOUND-OFF) EDGES OF STOCKINETTE STITCH

This type of seam is used to join shoulder seams.

1 Align the swatches with right sides facing up and the bound-off edges abutting each other with the stitches lined up.

2 Use safety pins or locking stitch markers to pin the pieces together, and start the seaming yarn as shown on page 103. Pass the threaded needle under the two legs of the "V" formed by a stitch inside of the bound-off edge.

3 Pass the threaded needle under the corresponding stitch inside of the bound-off edge on the opposite side. Pull the yarn tightly enough to make the bound-off edge roll to the inside and form a seam. Continue working from side to side until the seam has been joined. At the end of the seam, pass the threaded needle to the wrong side and make a back stitch or two in the seam. Finish by weaving in the ends securely.

1

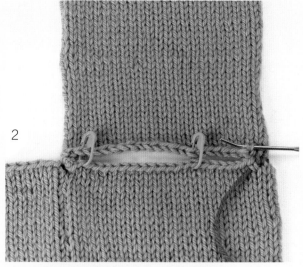

2

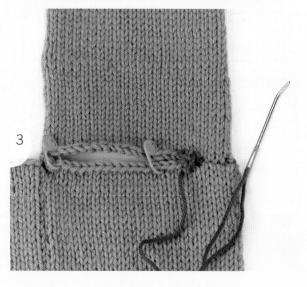

3

INVISIBLE SEAM FOR WEAVING A VERTICAL (SIDE) EDGE TO A HORIZONTAL (BOUND-OFF) EDGE OF STOCKINETTE STITCH

This type of seam is used to join stitches to rows such as joining the top of a sleeve to an armhole or shoulder edge.

1 Align the swatches with right sides facing up and the bound-off edge of one swatch abutting the side edge of the other.

2 Use safety pins or locking stitch markers to pin the pieces together and start the seaming yarn as shown on page 103. Pass the threaded needle under one or two bars on the side edge.*

3 Pass the threaded needle under the two legs of the "V" formed by a stitch inside of the boundoff edge.

4 Continue working side to side from rows to stitches. At the end of the seam, pass the threaded needle to the wrong side and make a back stitch or two in the seam. Finish by weaving in the ends securely.

*Since there are more rows than stitches, it will be necessary to compensate by occasionally passing the threaded needle under two bars on the side edge instead of one.

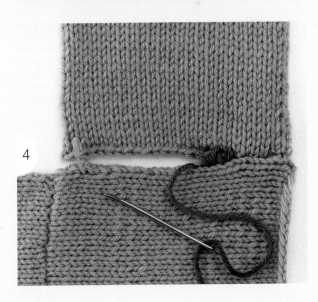

DIRECTIONAL BLOCKS SCARF

The unique characteristics of self-striping yarn are used create a scarf with directional blocks. This scarf is made by knitting a narrow center panel and then adding long strips along the sides and finishing with small strips at each narrow end. The technique is somewhat like making a quilt and it can be used with self-striping yarns as shown, but it would also be very effective with different colors.

MATERIALS

YARN
- medium weight self-striping yarn, approx. 310 yd (283.5 m)

NEEDLES AND NOTIONS
- US size 7 (4.5 mm) 9" (23 cm) single-pointed needles or size needed to achieve gauge
- US size 5 (3.75 mm) circular needle at least 32" (81 cm) long, or two sizes smaller than size needed to achieve gauge
- yarn needle for weaving in ends
- rustproof pins for blocking

EQUIPMENT
- iron
- ironing board

GAUGE

- 20 sts = 4" (10 cm) in stockinette stitch

FINISHED DIMENSIONS

- 6" (15 cm) wide by 51" (130 cm) long

SKILLS

- achieving different effects from the same self striping yarn
- joining blocks of knitting by picking up stitches

HOW TO KNIT THE DIRECTIONAL BLOCKS SCARF

1 Knit center panel Using larger needle, cast on 17 sts.

Row 1 (RS): Knit.

Row 2: Purl.

Repeat rows 1 and 2 (stockinette stitch) until length from cast-on edge is approximately 46" (117 cm). Bind off stitches.

2 Pick up stitches for first side block using the smaller needle. Position the center panel with the right side facing you and the length running from side to side. Starting from the right corner and using the smaller needle, pick up and knit 3 stitches for every 4 rows of knitting. Work across the entire long edge; you should have about 225 stitches. Don't worry if your stitch count varies by a few stitches. Your goal should be to pick up somewhere in the neighborhood of 225 stitches.

3 Knit side band. After picking up the stitches for the side band, work 16 rows in garter stitch (knit every row). Bind off from the wrong side. If you have a tendency to bind off tightly (your bound-off edges tend to curve), then use a needle one or two sizes larger for the bind-off needle.

Side Band	
Center Panel	End band

4 Repeat steps 2 and 3 for other side of center panel.

5 Pick up stitches for end bands. Position the scarf with the right side facing you and the short edge up. Starting from the right corner of the short edge of the side band, pick up and knit 8 stitches from the side band, 15 stitches from the center panel, and 8 stitches from the other side band. There should be a total of 31 stitches. When picking up stitches from the side bands, pick up 1 stitch from each garter ridge.

6 Knit end band. After picking up the stitches for the end band, work 16 rows in garter stitch (knit every row). Bind off from the wrong side.

7 Repeat steps 5 and 6 for other end.

8 Finish scarf by weaving in all loose ends and steam blocking following general directions on page 50.

5

BABY BATHROBE

Baby items make a terrific first garment. The knitting and finishing are quickly accomplished so the project isn't overwhelming. The other appeal is that the little pieces are always just so cute! This baby bathrobe would be the ultimate shower gift—useful yet unusual. It's made from bulky organic cotton that's both soft and absorbent.

MATERIALS

YARN

- 🧶 bulky weight yarn (preferably cotton or cotton acrylic blend) in two colors in approximate yardage as shown in chart on page 114

NEEDLES AND NOTIONS

- US size 9 (5.5 mm) 24" (61 cm) circular needle or size needed to achieve gauge for making body pieces*

- US size 7 (4.5 mm) 32" (81 cm) circular needle or two sizes smaller than size used to achieve gauge, for making seed stitch bands

- US size 7 (4.5 mm) 9" (23 cm) single-pointed needles or two sizes smaller than size used to achieve gauge, for making belt

- *The body pieces can be knit on single-pointed needles, but the circular needle is recommended since this yarn is quite heavy and circular needles will be easier on your hands and wrists.*

- yarn needle for weaving in ends

- locking stitch markers or straight pins

- two ½" to ¾" (1.5 to 2 cm) buttons

- sewing needle and thread

EQUIPMENT

- iron

- ironing board

GAUGE

- 14 sts = 4" (10 cm) in stockinette stitch

SKILLS

- choosing the correct size pattern

- shaping a "V" neck

- assembling a garment

- making seams in knit items

PATTERN SIZING

Clothing items are usually made with some ease, which is the difference between the actual measurements of the garment compared to the measurement of the body it is designed to fit. The baby bathrobe has an ease of 4" (10 cm); the actual garment chest measurement of the 12 month size is 24" (61 cm) even though the average chest measurement of a 12-month-old baby is 20" (51 cm).

This pattern is written for a range of sizes, so it will be necessary to determine which directions apply to the size you are making. The chart defines the dimensions of a particular size. It not only suggests the size (12 months, for instance) but also states the average chest size of a 12-month-old baby (20" [51 cm]). Please take note that the size numbers (1, 2, and 3) used in the chart and pattern are not the same as children's clothing sizes. This numbering system is used to make the patterns easier to read.

SIZES AND FINISHED DIMENSIONS

	SIZE 1	SIZE 2	SIZE 3
To Fit Size	12 month	18 month	24 month
To Fit Chest Size	20" (51 cm)	21" (53 cm)	22" (56 cm)
Actual Garment Chest Measurement	24" (61 cm)	25" (63.5 cm)	26" (66 cm)
Length	17" (43 cm)	19" (48 cm)	21" (53 cm)
Yardage Required Yarn A	275 yd (251 m)	320 yd (292 m)	365 yd (334 m)
Yardage Required Yarn B	110 yd (101 m)	130 yd (119 m)	145 yd (133 m)

○ Directions are shown as Size 1 (Size 2, Size 3). Note that the size numbers (1, 2, and 3) are not the same as children's clothing sizes. This numbering system is used to make the patterns

Below is a schematic of the individual pieces showing the finished dimensions of each piece. The measurements use the same organization as the directions: Size 1 (Size 2, Size 3)

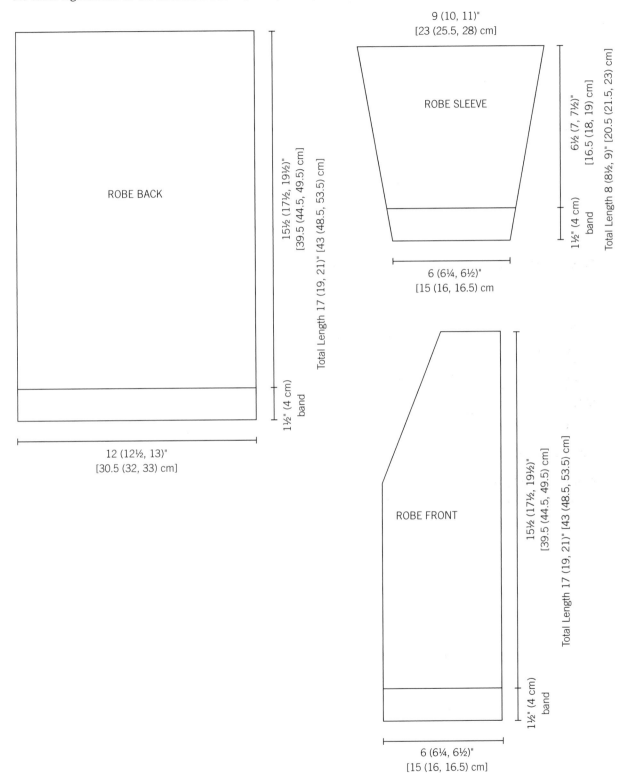

ROBE BACK

15½ (17½, 19½)"
[39.5 (44.5, 49.5) cm]

Total Length 17 (19, 21)" [43 (48.5, 53.5) cm]

1½" (4 cm) band

12 (12½, 13)"
[30.5 (32, 33) cm]

9 (10, 11)"
[23 (25.5, 28) cm]

ROBE SLEEVE

6½ (7, 7½)"
[16.5 (18, 19) cm]

Total Length 8 (8½, 9)" [20.5 (21.5, 23) cm]

1½" (4 cm) band

6 (6¼, 6½)"
[15 (16, 16.5) cm

ROBE FRONT

15½ (17½, 19½)"
[39.5 (44.5, 49.5) cm]

Total Length 17 (19, 21)" [43 (48.5, 53.5) cm]

1½" (4 cm) band

6 (6¼, 6½)"
[15 (16, 16.5) cm]

HOW TO MAKE THE BABY BATH ROBE

BACK

1 Using larger needle and yarn A cast on 42 (44, 46) sts. Purl the next row. See note on page 102 about using a row counter.

2 Work remainder of body in stockinette stitch as follows:

Row 1: Knit.
Row 2: Purl.
Repeat rows 1 and 2 until the length from the cast-on row is 15½" (17½", 19½ ") [39.5 cm (44.5 cm, 49.5 cm)]. Bind off and cut the yarn, leaving a tail at least 8" (20 cm) long.

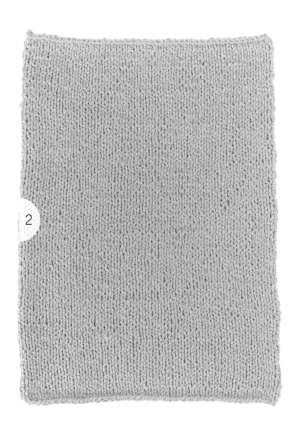

RIGHT FRONT

(You are making the right front as worn on the body.)

3 Using larger needle and yarn A cast on 21 (22, 23) sts. Purl the next row.

4 Work body in stockinette stitch as follows:

Row 1: Knit.
Row 2: Purl.
Repeat rows 1 and 2 until the length from the cast-on row is 11" (12½", 14") [28 cm (32 cm, 35.5 cm)]. Before beginning the neckline decreases below, be certain that you have just finished a purl row.

5 Decrease along neck edge. Note: rows 11 and 12 are skipped for size 1 because of its fewer number of stitches.

Row 1: K1, ssk, knit to end of row—20 (21, 22) sts remain.
Row 2: Purl.
Row 3: K1, ssk, knit to end of row—19 (20, 21) sts remain.
Row 4: Purl.
Row 5: K1, ssk, knit to end of row—18 (19, 20) sts remain.
Row 6: Purl.
Row 7: K1, ssk, knit to end of row—17 (18, 19) sts remain.
Row 8: Purl.
Row 9: K1, ssk, knit to end of row—16 (17, 18) sts remain.

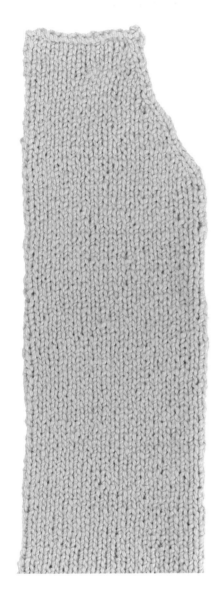

6

Row 10: Purl.

Row 11 for sizes 2 and 3 only (Skip this row for size 1): K1, ssk, knit to end of row—(16, 17) sts remain.

Row 12 for sizes 2 and 3 only (Skip this row for size 1): Purl.

Row 13: Knit.

Row 14: Purl.

Row 15: K1, ssk, knit to end of row—15 (15, 16) sts remain.

Row 16: Purl.

Row 17: Knit.

Row 18: Purl.

6 Repeat rows 17 and 18 until the length from the cast-on edge is 15½" (17½", 19½") [39.5 cm (44.5 cm, 49.5 cm]). Bind off and cut the yarn, leaving a tail at least 8" (20 cm) long.

(continued)

LEFT FRONT

(You are making the left front as worn on the body.)

7 Using larger needle and yarn A cast on 21 (22, 23) sts. Purl the next row.

8 Work body as follows:

Row 1: Knit.
Row 2: Purl.
Repeat rows 1 and 2 until the length from the cast-on row is 11" (12½", 14") [28 cm (32 cm, 35.5 cm]). Before beginning the neckline decreases below, be certain that you have just finished a purl row.

9 Decrease along neck edge. Note: rows 11 and 12 are skipped for size 1 because of its fewer number of stitches.

Row 1: Knit until 3 sts remain, k2tog, k1—20 (21, 22) sts remain.
Row 2: Purl.
Row 3: Knit until 3 sts remain, k2tog, k1—19 (20, 21) sts remain.
Row 4: Purl.
Row 5: Knit until 3 sts remain, k2tog, k1—18 (19, 20) sts remain.
Row 6: Purl.
Row 7: Knit until 3 sts remain, k2tog, k1—17 (18, 19) sts remain.
Row 8: Purl.
Row 9: Knit until 3 sts remain, k2tog, k1—16 (17, 18) sts remain.
Row 10: Purl.
Row 11 for sizes 2 and 3 only (Skip this row for size 1): Knit until 3 sts remain, k2tog, k1—(16, 17) sts remain.
Row 12 for sizes 2 and 3 only (Skip this row for size 1): Purl.
Row 13: Knit.
Row 14: Purl.

Row 15: Knit until 3 sts remain, k2tog, k1—15 (15, 16) sts remain.
Row 16: Purl.
Row 17: Knit.
Row 18: Purl.

10 Repeat rows 17 and 18 until the length from the cast-on edge is 15½" (17½", 19½") [39.5 cm (44.5 cm, 49.5 cm]). Bind off and cut the yarn leaving a tail at least 8" (20 cm) long.

SLEEVES (MAKE TWO)

11 Cuff: using smaller needle and yarn B, cast on 23 (23, 25) sts. When making cast-on row, leave a tail at least 10" (25.5 cm) long that will later be used to seam the cuff. Work cuff in seed stitch as follows:

Row 1: *K1, p1*; repeat from * to * until 1 st remains, k1.
Repeat row 1 eight more times for a total of 9 rows.

12 Sleeve shaping: shape sleeves by working increases along each edge. From this point, each sleeve has a unique set of directions. Follow the directions for the size you are making.

SIZE 1
Change to larger needles and yarn A.
Row 1: K11, k2tog, k10—22 sts remain.
Row 2: Purl.
Row 3: Knit.
Row 4: Purl.
Row 5: K1, M1R, knit until 1 st remains, M1L, k1—24 sts.
Row 6: Purl.
Row 7: Knit.
Row 8: Purl.
Row 9: K1, M1R, knit until 1 st remains, M1L, k1—26 sts.
Row 10: Purl.
Row 11: Knit.
Row 12: Purl.
Row 13: Knit.
Row 14: Purl.
Row 15: K1, M1R, knit until 1 st remains, M1L, k1—28 sts.
Rows 16 to 21: Repeat rows 11 to 15—30 sts after completing row 21.
Rows 22 to 27: Repeat rows 11 to 15—32 sts after completing row 27.

After completing row 32, the length from the cast-on row should be 8" (20 cm). If necessary, add or subtract rows after the last increase (row 27) in order to reach the correct length.
Row 28: Purl.
Row 29: Knit.
Row 30: Purl.
Row 31: Knit.
Row 32: Purl.
Bind off and cut the yarn, leaving a tail at least 8" (20 cm) long.

SIZE 2
Change to larger needles and yarn A.
Row 1: K11, k2tog, k10—22 sts remain.
Row 2: Purl.
Row 3: Knit.
Row 4: Purl.
Row 5: K1, M1R, knit until 1 st remains, M1L, k1—24 sts.
Row 6: Purl.
Row 7: Knit.
Row 8: Purl.
Row 9: K1, M1R, knit until 1 st remains, M1L, k1—26 sts.
Rows 10 to 13: Repeat rows 6 to 9—28 sts after completing row 13.
Rows 14 to 17: Repeat rows 6 to 9—30 sts after completing row 17.
Rows 18 to 21: Repeat rows 6 to 9—32 sts after completing row 21.
Rows 22 to 25: Repeat rows 6 to 9—34 sts after completing row 25.
Row 26: Purl.
Row 27: Knit.
Row 28: Purl.
Row 29: Knit.
Row 30: Purl.
Row 31: K1, M1R, knit until 1 st remains, M1L, k1—36 sts.

(continued)

After completing row 36, length from the cast-on row should be 8½" (21.5 cm). If necessary, add or subtract rows after the last increase (row 31) in order to reach the correct length.

Row 32: Purl.

Row 33: Knit.

Row 34: Purl.

Row 35: Knit.

Row 36: Purl.

Bind off and cut the yarn, leaving a tail at least 8" (20 cm) long.

SIZE 3

Change to larger needles and yarn A.

Row 1: K11, k2tog, k10—24 sts remain.

Row 2: Purl.

Row 3: Knit.

Row 4: Purl.

Row 5: K1, M1R, knit until 1 st remains, M1L, k1—26 sts.

Row 6: Purl.

Row 7: Knit.

Row 8: Purl.

Row 9: K1, M1R, knit until 1 st remains, M1L, k1—28 sts.

Rows 10 to 13: Repeat rows 6 to 9—30 sts after completing row 13.

Rows 14 to 17: Repeat rows 6 to 9—32 sts after completing row 17.

Rows 18 to 21: Repeat rows 6 to 9—34 sts after completing row 21.

Row 22: Purl.

Row 23: Knit.

Row 24: Purl.

Row 25: Knit.

Row 26: Purl.

Row 27: K1, M1R, knit until 1 st remains, M1L, k1—36 sts.

Rows 28 to 33: Repeat rows 22 to 27—38 sts after completing row 21.

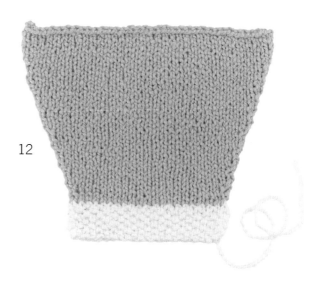

12

After completing row 38, the length from the cast-on row should be 9" (23 cm). If necessary, add or subtract rows after the last increase (row 33) in order to reach the correct length.

Row 34: Purl.

Row 35: Knit.

Row 36: Purl.

Row 37: Knit.

Row 38: Purl.

Bind off and cut the yarn, leaving a tail at least 8" (20 cm) long.

Lightly steam all pieces following directions on page 50. The pieces should be as smooth and flat as possible and the measurements should conform to those shown in the schematics on page 115.

HOW TO ASSEMBLE THE ROBE

13 The robe pieces will be joined in stages. After each seam is completed, steam it lightly to ensure that it lies as flat as possible before the next piece is joined.

14 Begin by joining the fronts to the back at the shoulder seam. Align the left front so that the bound-off edge adjoins the bound-off edge of the shoulder and pin to secure with locking stitch markers or straight pins. The selvedge edges should be lined up on the right side and the neck shaping should face to the left.

15 Cut a length of yarn A about 18" (45.5 cm) long and thread onto a yarn needle. Sew the shoulder seam together using the mattress stitch for bound-off edges (page 106). Leave a tail at least 8" (20 cm) long at the beginning and remove pins as you work. When the seam is finished weave, in the ends to secure.

16 Align the right front to mirror the left front and join the shoulder seam.

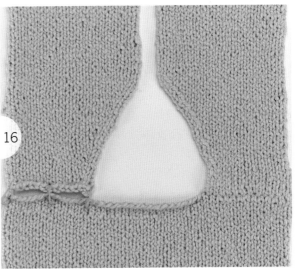

17 Mark the center point of the bound-off top edge of the sleeve.

18 Align the center with the shoulder seam. Pin the sleeve to the front and back sides. The distance from the sleeve center point to the sleeve side edge should be 4½" (5", 5⅜") [11.5 cm (12.5 cm, 13.5 cm).

(continued)

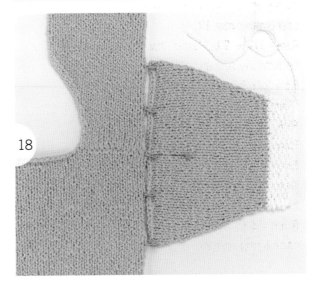

19 Cut a length of yarn A about 18" (45.5 cm) long and thread on to a yarn needle. Join the sleeve to the body using the mattress stitch for bound-off edges to side edges (page 107). Leave a tail at least 8" (20 cm) long at the beginning and remove pins as you work. When the seam is finished, weave in the ends to secure.

20 Repeat for other sleeve.

21 Working one side at a time, pin the front to the back to make a seam and pin the sleeve edges to make a seam. The underarm and side will be sewn as one continuous seam.

22 Cut a length of yarn A about 30" (76 cm) long and thread on to a yarn needle. Sew the seam using the mattress stitch for side edges (page 104). Begin sewing on the sleeve seam above the cuff. Leave a tail at least 8" (20 cm) long at the beginning and remove pins as you work. When the seam is finished, weave in the ends to secure.

23 Using the long tail from the cast-on of the cuff, join the short cuff seam. Work from side to side in a modified mattress stitch: catching the purl bumps that are on the selvedge edge, which gives a flatter seam that won't be seen when the cuffs are turned up. When the seam is finished, weave in the ends to secure.

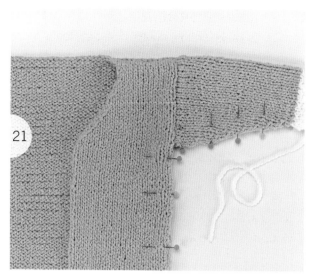

21

23

CONTRAST BORDER

24 To make bottom contrast border, pick up stitches from the cast-on edge beginning with the center edge of the left front. As a basic guide, pick up approximately 1 stitch for each cast-on stitch on the edge. It isn't necessary to pick up exactly the same number as suggested in the guide below. Just be certain you have an odd number of stitches after all the stitches have been picked up. If not, simply adjust the spacing between the last few stitches (either one stitch closer or further away). Pick up stitches as follows:

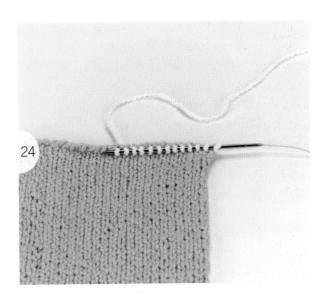

Size 1: Total of 81 sts: 20 from left front, 41 from back, 20 from right front.
Size 2: Total of 85 sts: 21 from left front, 43 from back, 21 from right front.
Size 3: Total of 89 sts: 22 from left front, 45 from back, 22 from right front.

25 Work band in seed stitch as follows:

Row 1: *K1, p1*; repeat from * to * until 1 st remains, k1.
Repeat row 1 seven more times for a total of 8 rows. Bind off in pattern. Cut yarn, leaving a tail at least 8" (20 cm) long.

26 Stitches are picked up for the continuous band that is attached to the center front and neck edges. It isn't necessary to pick up exactly the same number as suggested in the guide on page 124. Just be certain you have an odd number of stitches after all the stitches have been picked up. If not, simply adjust the spacing between the last few stitches (either 1 row closer or further away).

(continued)

When making the center front and neck edge border, pick up stitches from the side (selvedge edge) beginning with the bottom corner of the right center front **(A)**. As a general guide, pick up about 5 stitches for every 8 rows along the center front. The best way to determine the spacing of the picked up stitches along the angled portion of the neck shaping is to divide the distance in half (or even quarters) and mark with pins. When picking up stitches along this edge, divide the number to be picked up among the sections marked with the pins. The neck edge includes the space taken up by the shoulder seams **(B)**. Along the back of the neck, pick up approximately 1 stitch for each bound-off stitch **(C)**. Pick up stitches as follows:

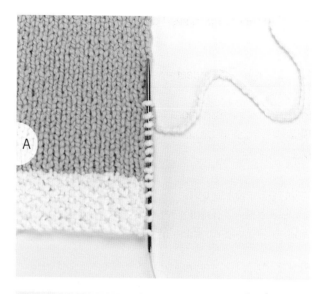

Size 1: Total of 141 sts: 45 from right center front, 19 from right angled neck line, 14 from center back, 19 from left angled neck line, and 44 from left center front.

Size 2: Total of 157 sts: 49 from right center front, 22 from right angled neck line, 16 from center back, 22 from left angled neck line, and 48 from left center front.

Size 3: Total of 171 sts: 54 from right center front, 24 from right angled neck line, 16 from center back, 24 from left angled neck line, and 53 from left center front.

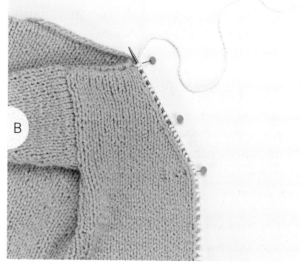

27 Work band in seed stitch as follows:

Row 1: *K1, p1*; repeat from * to * until 1 st remains, k1.
Repeat row 1 seven more times for a total of 8 rows. Bind off in pattern. Cut yarn leaving a tail at least 8" (20 cm) long.

28 Make the belt. Using the smaller single-pointed needles and yarn B, cast on 6 sts. Work the belt in rib stitch as follows:

Row 1: *K1, p1*; repeat from * to * to end of row.
Repeat row 1 until the belt is 36" (37", 38") [91.5 cm (94 cm, 96.5 cm)] long. Bind off in pattern and cut yarn, leaving a tail at least 8" (20 cm) long. Weave in all ends.

29 Lay the robe out so the back is flat and smooth. With a straight pin, mark a distance on each side seam that is 7" (7½", 8") [18 cm (19 cm, 20 cm)] down from the shoulder seam. Measuring between these two marks, find the center back and mark it with a straight pin.

30 Position the center of the belt on the center back and be certain that the belt is parallel to the bottom and centered widthwise over the marks on the side seam. Pin the center and then pin 3" (7.5 cm) to each side of center.

31 Thread about 18" (45.5 cm) of yarn A on yarn needle. Knot the yarn and use a running stitch to attach the belt securely at each position which is marked 3" (7.5 cm) to the side of the center back.

32 Use sewing thread and needle to attach buttons.

33 Gently steam all bands and seams a final time. Sew in all loose ends.

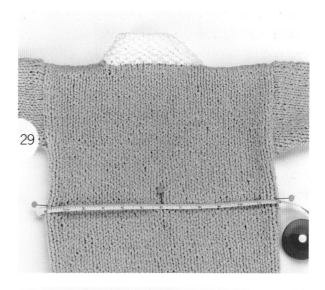

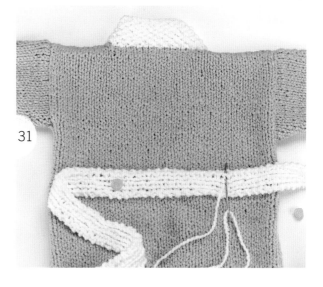

abbreviations

Here is the list of standard abbreviations used for knitting. Until you can readily identify them, keep the list handy whenever you knit.

BO	bind off (p. 20)		**Rev St st**	reverse stockinette stitch
BOR	beginning of round		**rm**	remove marker
cm	centimeter		**RS**	right side
CO	cast on		**WS**	wrong side
dpn(s)	double pointed needles		**sl**	slip
g	gram		**sm**	slip marker
K, k	knit		**ssk**	slip, slip, knit
k2tog	knit two together		**st**	stitch
kf&b	knit front and back		**sts**	stitches
LYS	local yarn shop		**St st**	stockinette stitch
m	meter		**wyib**	with yarn in back
mm	millimeter		**wyif**	with yarn in front
M1L	make one left		**yd**	yard(s)
M1R	make one right		**yo**	yarnover
P, p	purl		*** ***	repeat instructions between * as directed
p2tog	purl two together			
pf&b	purl front and back		**[ ]**	repeat instructions enclosed by brackets as directed
pm	place marker			
psso	pass slipped stitch over		**"**	inch(es)

about the author

Carri Hammett is a knitwear designer and writer who got her start by designing for customers in the yarn shop she opened in 2002. She loves to collaborate with both readers and customers as together they express their love of knitting and expand their knitting knowledge and skill.

Carri sold her shop in 2010 so she could focus her energy on writing and expanding her online sales. She is also the author of *Scarves and Shawls for Yarn Lovers, Mittens and Hats for Yarn Lovers, Knitting 101* and *Ready, Set, Knit Cables*. Carri lives in Minnesota.

index

DON'T MISS THE OTHER BOOKS IN THE SERIES!

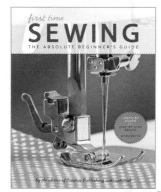

First Time Sewing
ISBN: 978-1-58923-804-6

MORE BOOKS ON KNITTING

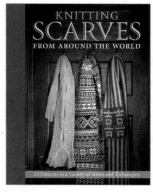

Knitting Scarves from Around the World
Edited by Kari Cornell
ISBN: 978-0-76034-064-6

Knitting 101
Carri Hammett
ISBN: 978-1-58923-646-2

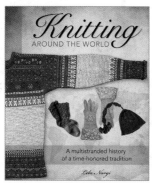

Knitting Around the World
Lela Nargi
ISBN: 978-0-76034-708-9

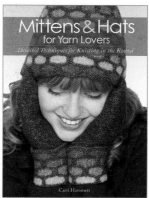

Mittens and Hats for Yarn Lovers
Carri Hammett
ISBN: 978-1-58923-575-5

The Complete Photo Guide to Knitting, 2nd Edition
Margaret Hubert
ISBN: 978-1-58923-820-6

Knitting Clothes Kids Love
Kate Oates
Nancy Langdon
ISBN: 978-1-58923-675-2